AF266687

Aurora Books, an imprint of Eco-Justice Press, L.L.C.

Aurora Books
P.O. Box 5409 Eugene, OR 97405
www.ecojusticepress.com

The Tiny Art Gallery: A Community Art Project
By David Diethelm

Library of Congress Control Number: 2017915871
ISBN 978-1-945432-17-0

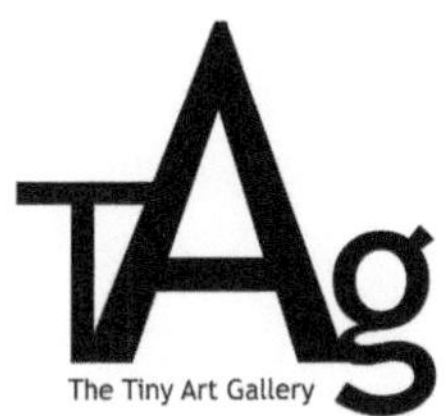

The Tiny Art Gallery
A Community Art Project

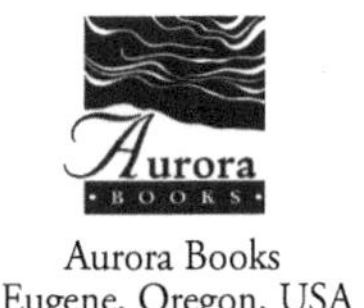

Aurora Books
Eugene, Oregon, USA

Introduction

I had a radical idea: a neighborhood gallery for people to display their artwork, and for others to borrow it. The borrowers could also interact with the artist by posting pictures of how they showed and appreciated the art in their homes.

The idea for the Tiny Art Gallery (TAG) started as a recurrent thought in the middle of the night. It kept coming back and waking me up for about a week to contemplate. A gallery with similar qualities to the 'Little Free Library' seemed to fit the persistent late night idea. The notion that art could be shared like books seemed quite exciting – usually art is coveted. So this was obviously not going to be a traditional gallery – they don't let you borrow canvas, brush and paints. And it was going to be more involved than a 'Little Free Library'.

Limitations on space required it be limited to small pieces of art. To include those without art experience, there would have to be art supplies for people to borrow, and a way to keep the project supplied. Obviously people needed to know about it, so reaching out to the neighborhood to get them involved was necessary, otherwise there wouldn't be any art. Ultimately, I also wanted to reach people beyond the immediate neighborhood.

I had to think of a name for the Gallery, and 'The Tiny Art Gallery' seemed right. It certainly is descriptive, so that's what it is.

The idea of interaction between the artist and the people borrowing the art led to the need for a website with pictures of the art in the TAG, and also pictures of the art being shown in the borrowers' homes. This seemed like something fun and unique to the TAG.

I put a note on an on-line neighborhood forum (nextdoor.com), and received quite a bit of positive feedback and interest in the idea. So, I continued to think about how to integrate the art with the supplying and funding needs. I started an on-line funding page on (Patreon.com) and a couple people began funding the project.

Being a publisher, the idea of a book to record the art displayed in the gallery and taken home and shown, seemed an obvious choice, hence this book. Made with the assistance of the fine patrons who donated funds to the project.

Thank you!

Getting Started

The purchase of the box for the Tiny Art Gallery (TAG) was the first big decision. It couldn't be too small, or to big, and not too expensive. I settled on a pre-made 'cupboard' from an on-line garden retailer. It seemed like a nice design, and wasn't very expensive. It would fit in and not be too obvious.

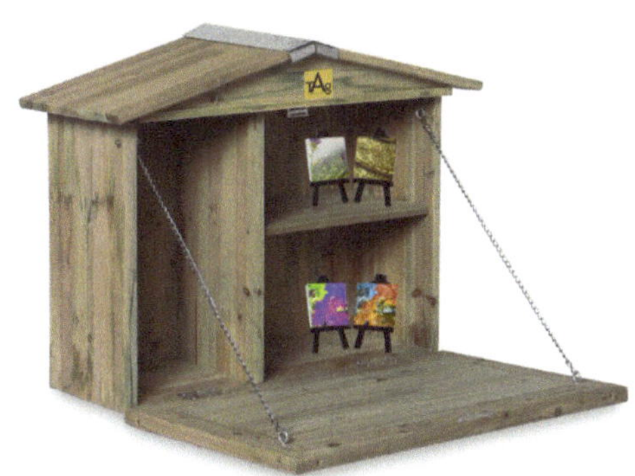

I mocked-up some tiny virtual pieces of art in Photoshop to put in the not-yet-delivered gallery. I used this image to get the initial word out to neighbors about the idea.

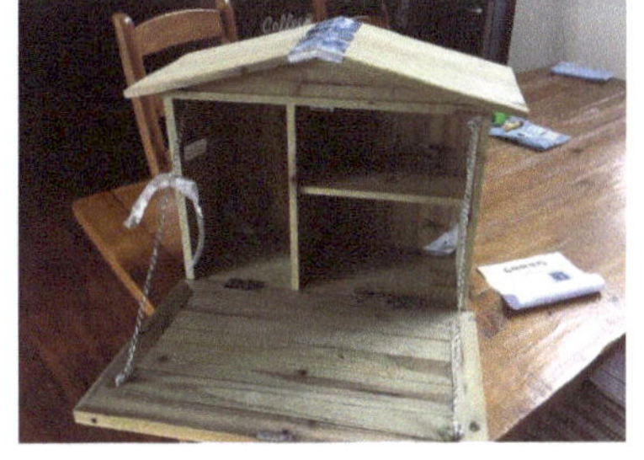

And then it arrived, and looked pretty good.

Next the first purchase of canvases, paints and brushes arrived. Which meant that it was time to dig a hole to put the post in for mounting the Tiny Art Gallery.

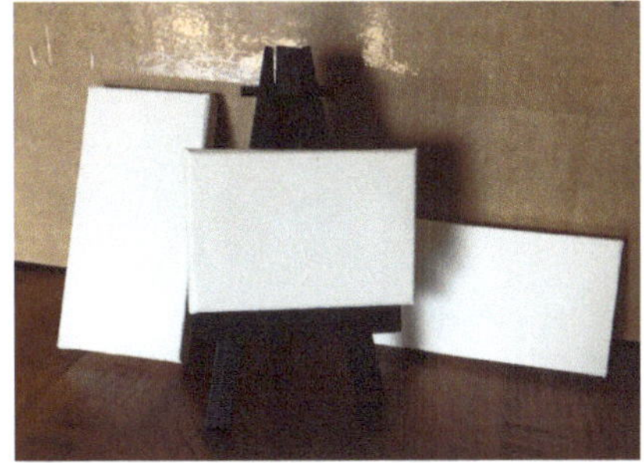

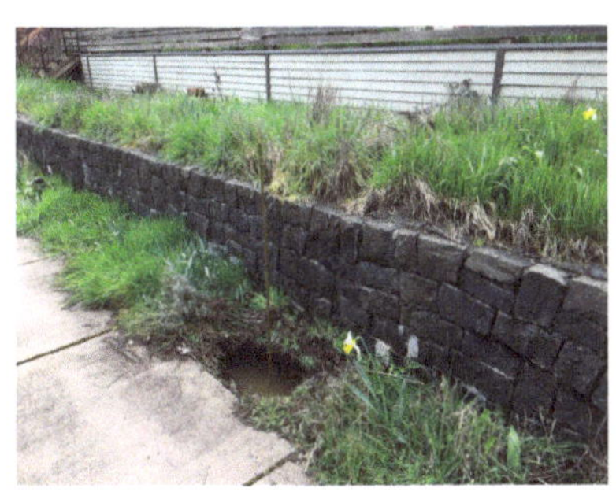

And, because it's Oregon, it rained a lot.

Then it was time to get the post installed. Many thanks to Brad for building the posts to match existing ones in the fence and mailbox, then installing the post, and attaching the Tiny Art Gallery to the top. It looks quite nice, even with overgrown grass around it.

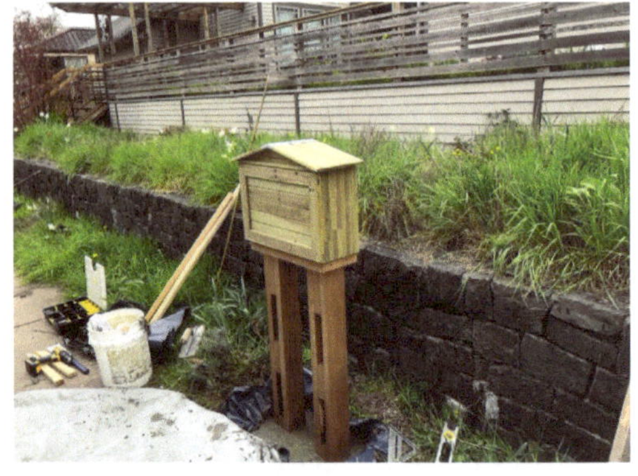

Nearly ready to open. Some neighbors are already interested.

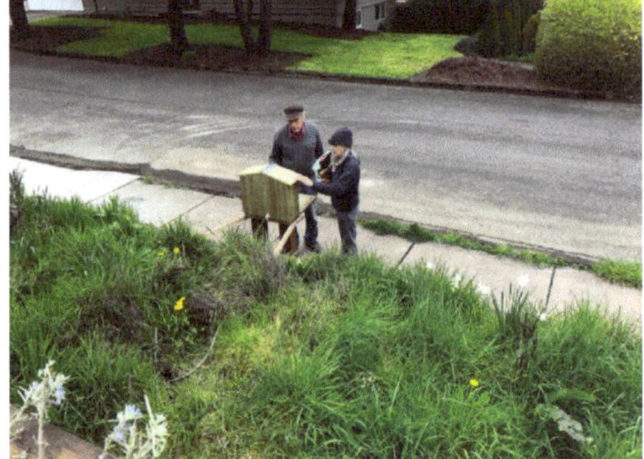

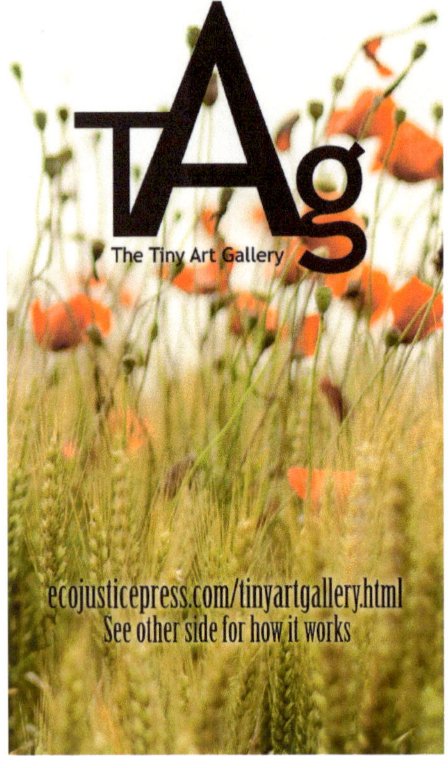

I made Business card sized information cards for inside the TAG with instructions on how to use the Gallery.

How it works

Read about it online:
ecojusticepress.com/tinyartgallery.html

Make Art:
• Borrow art supplies (please return) and make some art.
• Show your tiny art in the Tiny Art Gallery.
   It will also be shown on the website:
   ecojusticepress.com/tinyartgallery.html
   and included in a book, depending on funding.

Borrow Art:
• Borrow a pice of art and easel to show at home - please return
• Take a picture of it at your home show and email to:
   tag@ecojusticepress.com It will be posted on the website.

To Donate:
• Donate art supplies directly. Contact: tag@ecojusticepress.com
   or through patreon.com/tinyartgallery (as little as $1/month)

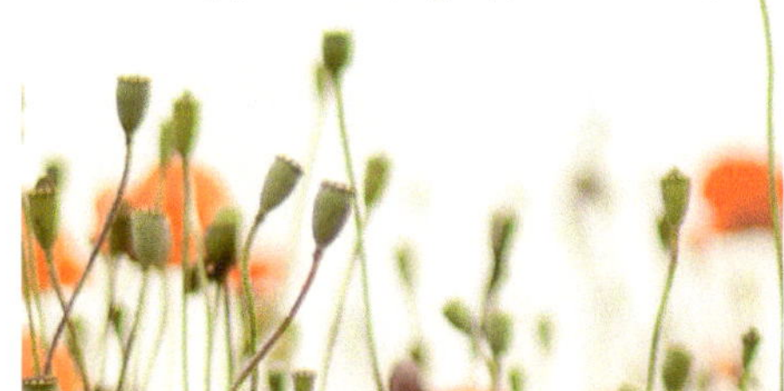

The Website

The website is an important part of the Tiny Art Gallery, it connects artists with those who directly enjoy their art. It also allows people farther away to experience, in some way, the art in the TAG.

Starting out, it made sense to add the Tiny Art Gallery as a page on the existing website for Eco-Justice Press. Being a small project it didn't require its own website. I put together a page about the TAG, and a page for the artwork — both in the TAG and from borrowed art. Working out the logistics of taking pictures and easily uploading them to the two galleries took a little work. Fortunately I heard about an application called Workflow. It easily creates an app made up of a series of actions chosen by the user. I made one so I can walk out to the Gallery, take a photo, crop it, run the Workflow app with the series of actions I want (select the image, resize, upload to Drop Box). It streamlined the process making it more about the art, and less the technology.

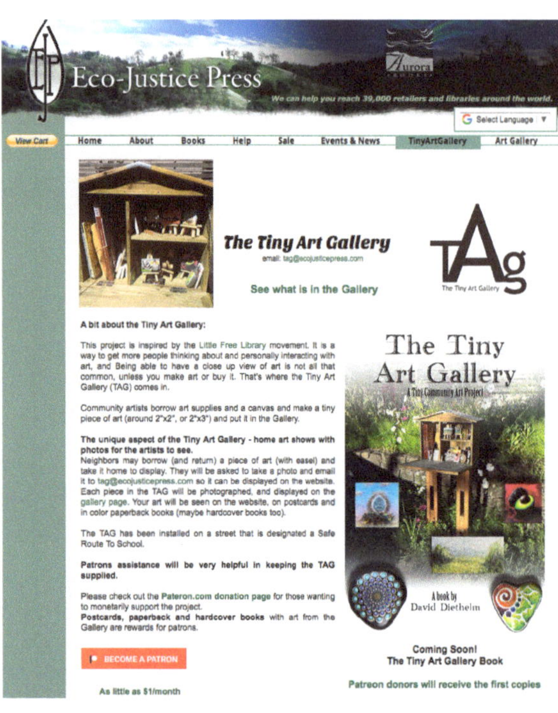

A view of the website in the Fall, announcing the book.

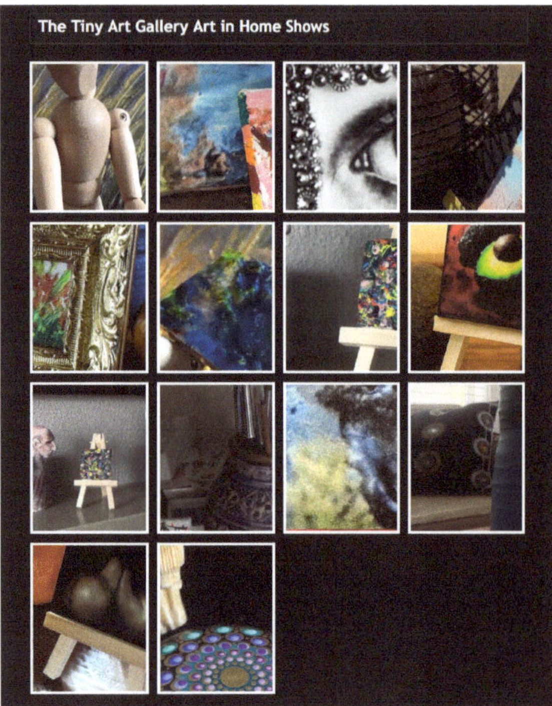

A view of the images people have shared of art they have borrowed.

The Opening

Easter morning 2017 was the official opening of the Tiny Art Gallery. The night before, I had put out supplies and a couple pieces of art that I had made. By 9:00 am, someone had already borrowed some paints, a brush, and a canvas. When I went to check later in the morning, there were three new pieces in the Gallery - two paintings and a painted rock. A good start, I was encouraged.

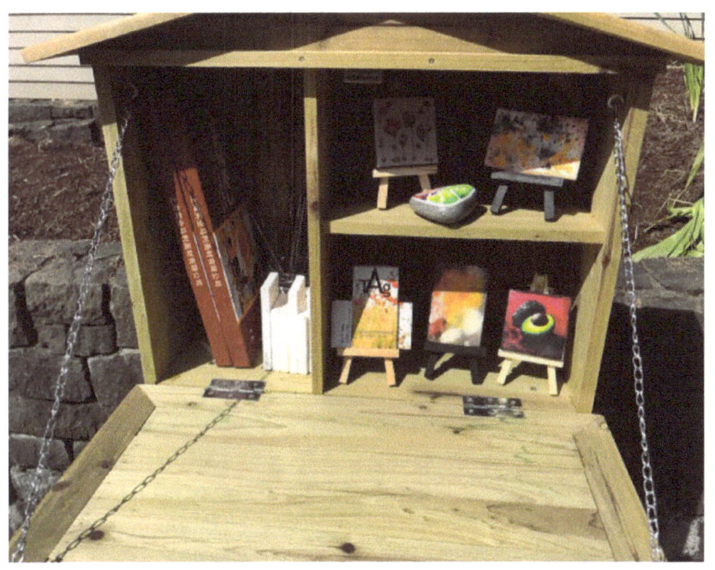

Here are the first pieces left on opening day.

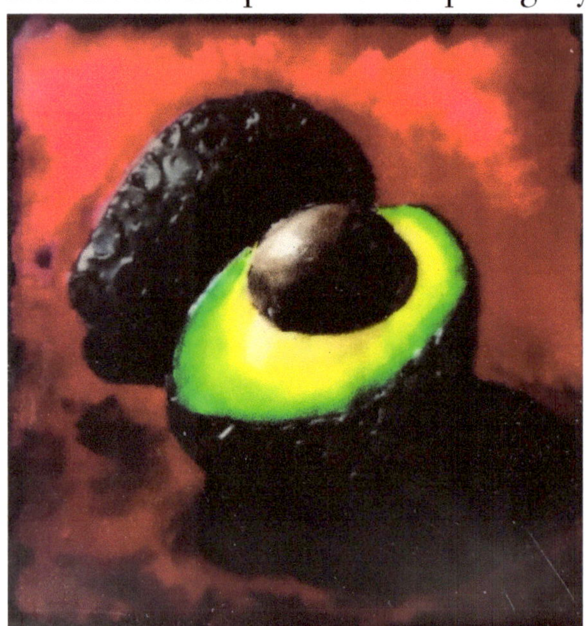
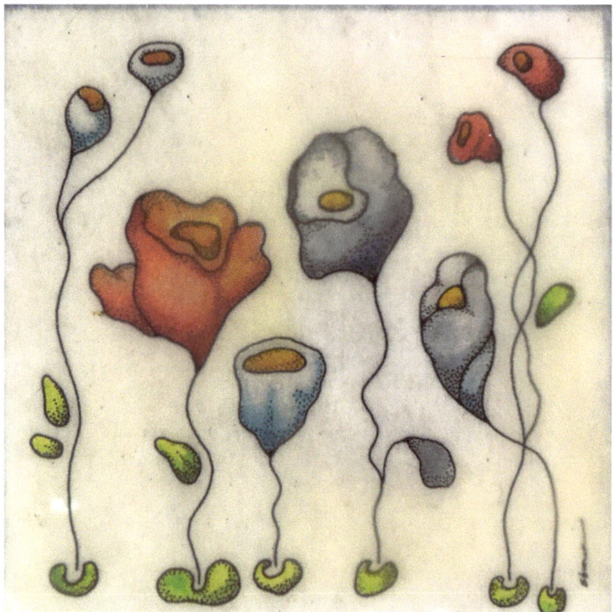
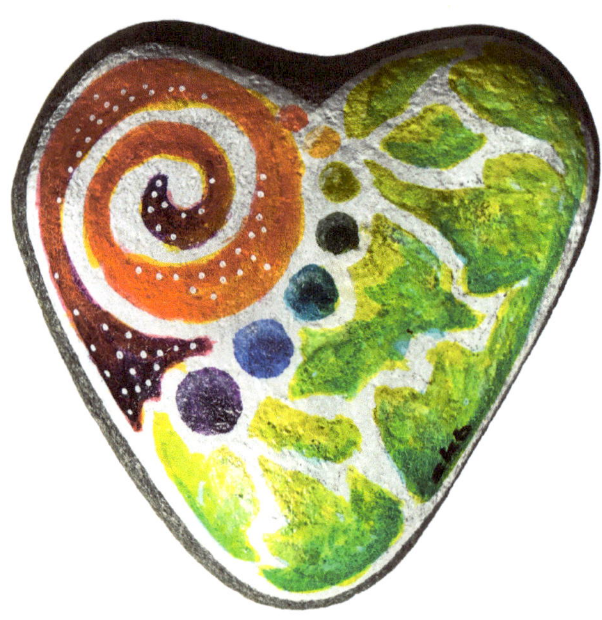

April and May Art

These are the pieces from the month and a half after the opening. I was contacted by the local newspaper, expressing interest in doing an article about the Tiny Art Gallery, once it's up and running for a while. Enough time to give the flowers around the TAG a bit of time to grow. I've attempted to transplant some very nice Russian sage to the area behind the TAG, we will see how much survives the uprooting and replanting.

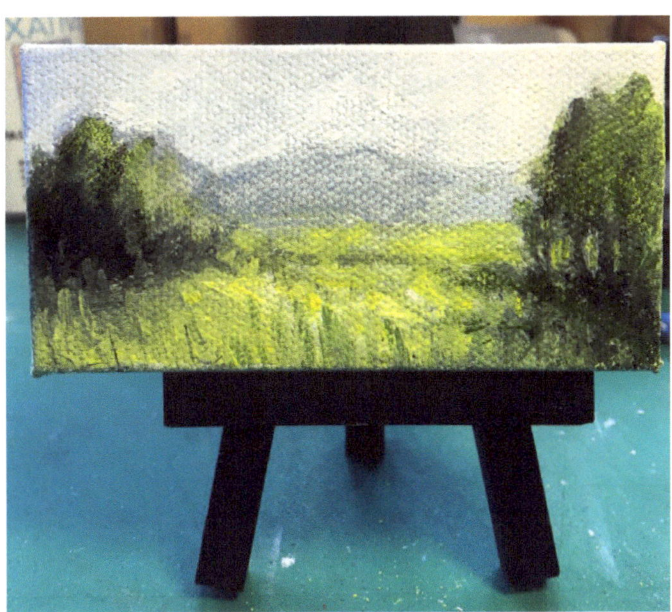

A painting of mine.

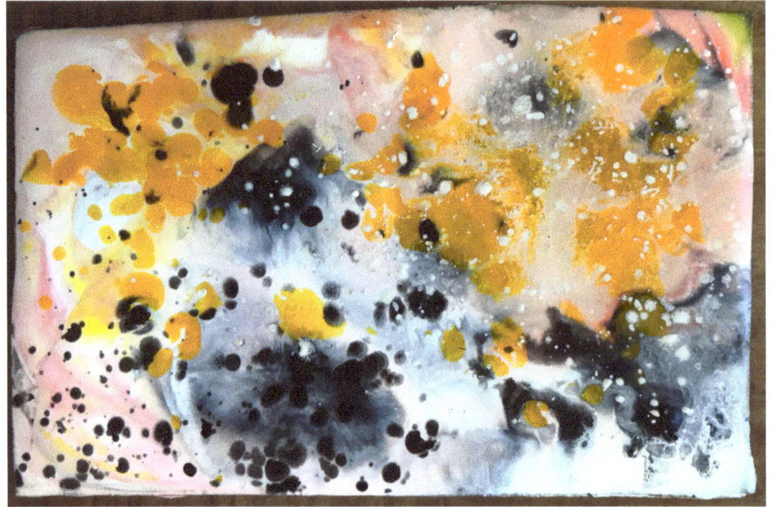

Two encasustics.

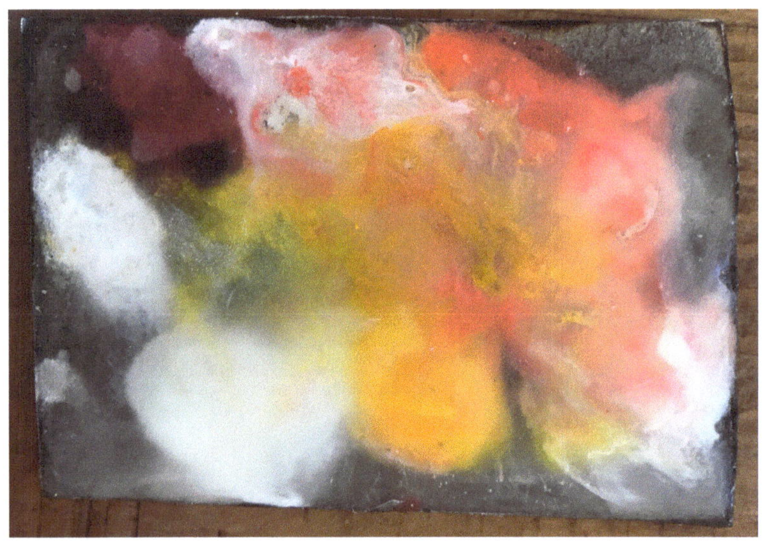

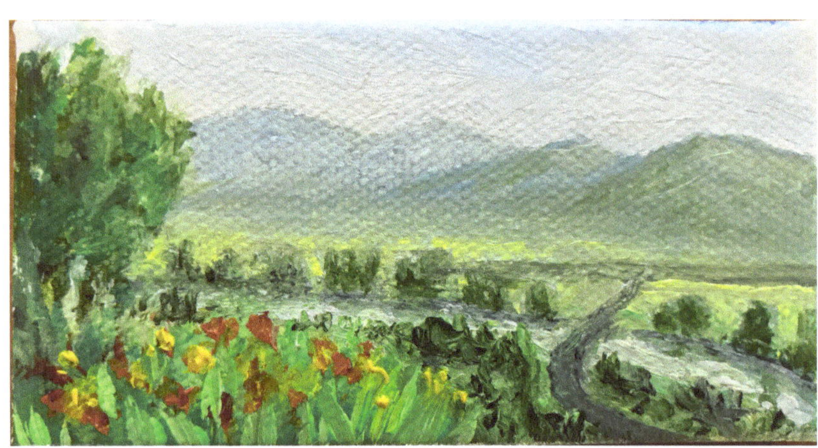

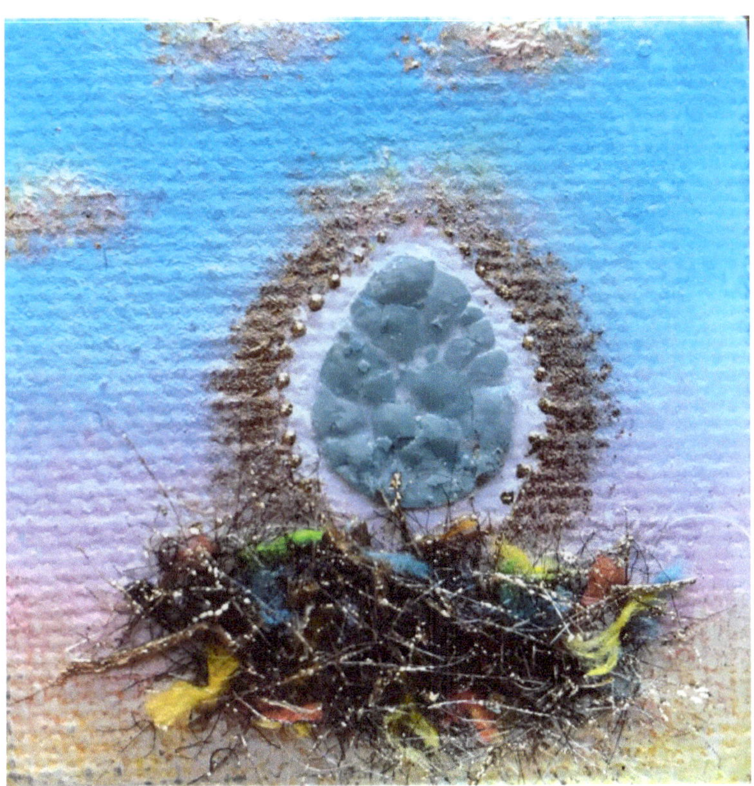

A wonderful piece by
neighbor Rebecca.

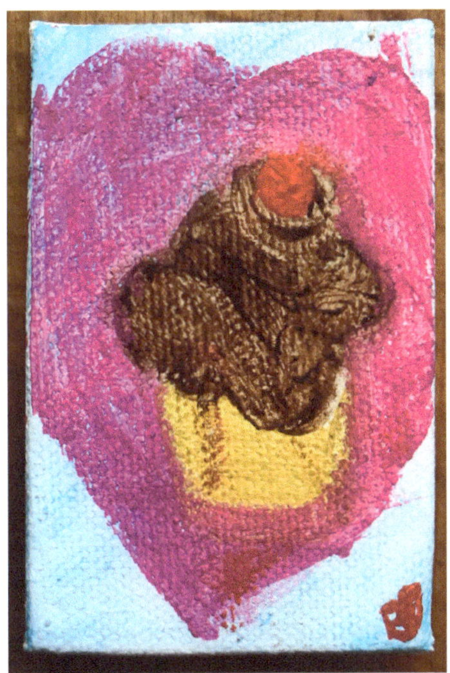

Cupcake!

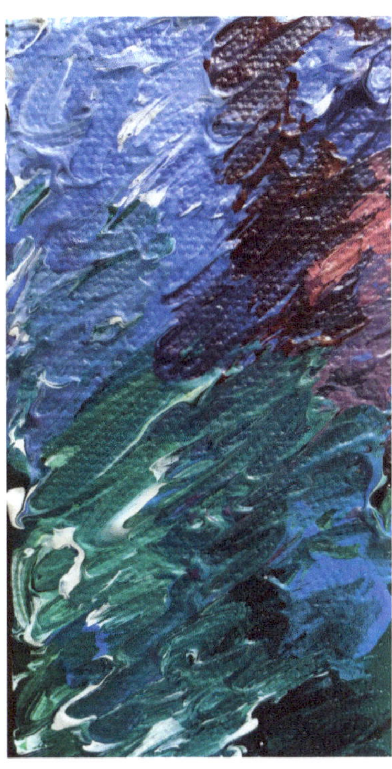

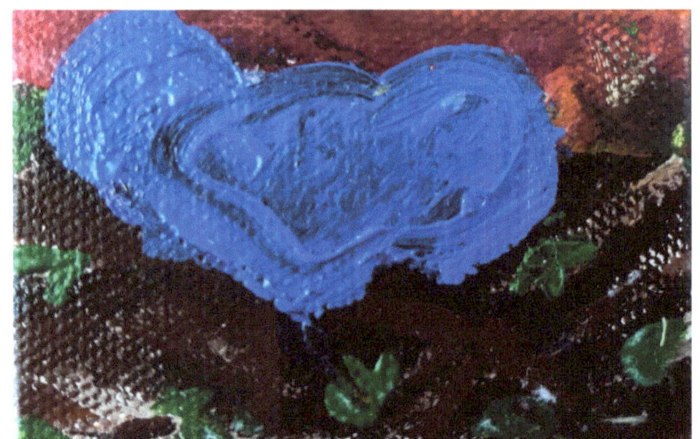

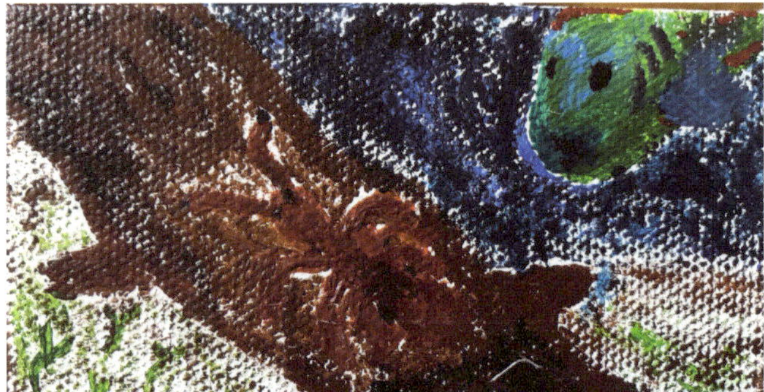

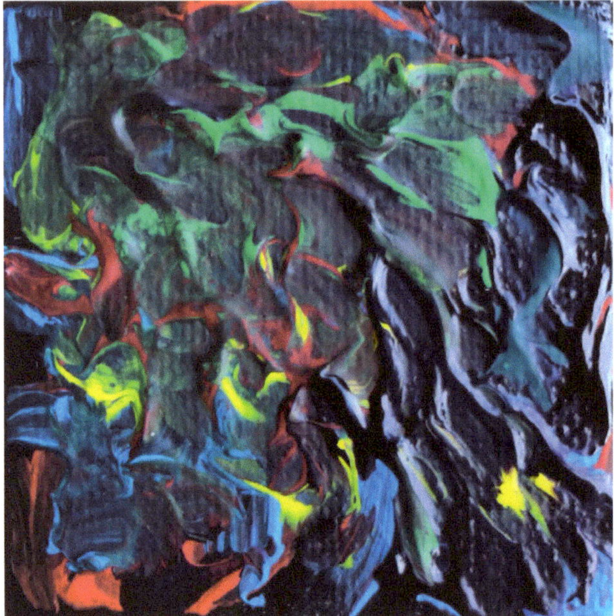

Fun textures and colors!

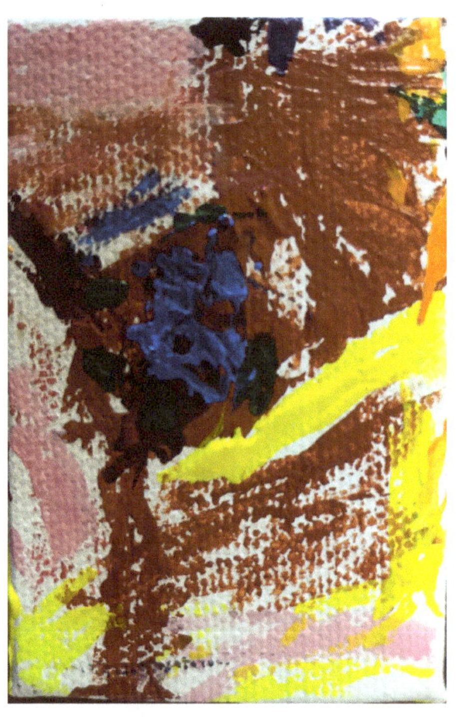

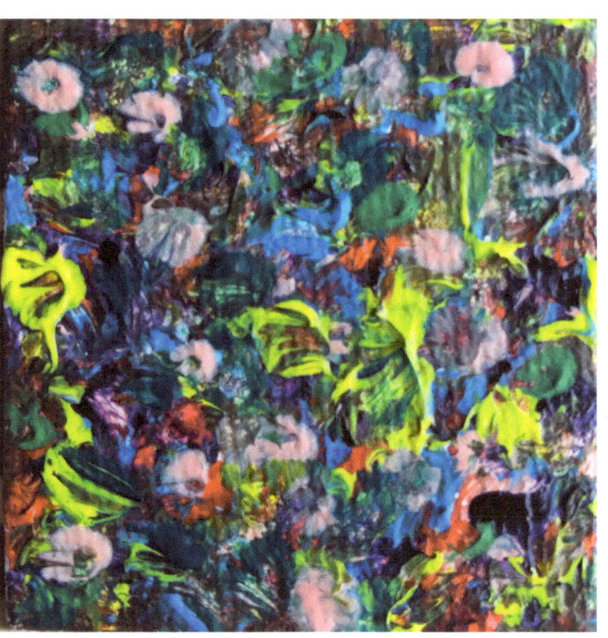

June Art

Another painted rock has arrived in the Tiny Art Gallery! Eugene, being what it is, you seem to meet the people you need to meet. Nicole paints wonderful rocks (now full-time). She really liked the idea of the TAG, and donated a beautiful piece. It has been borrowed and has traveled quite a bit.

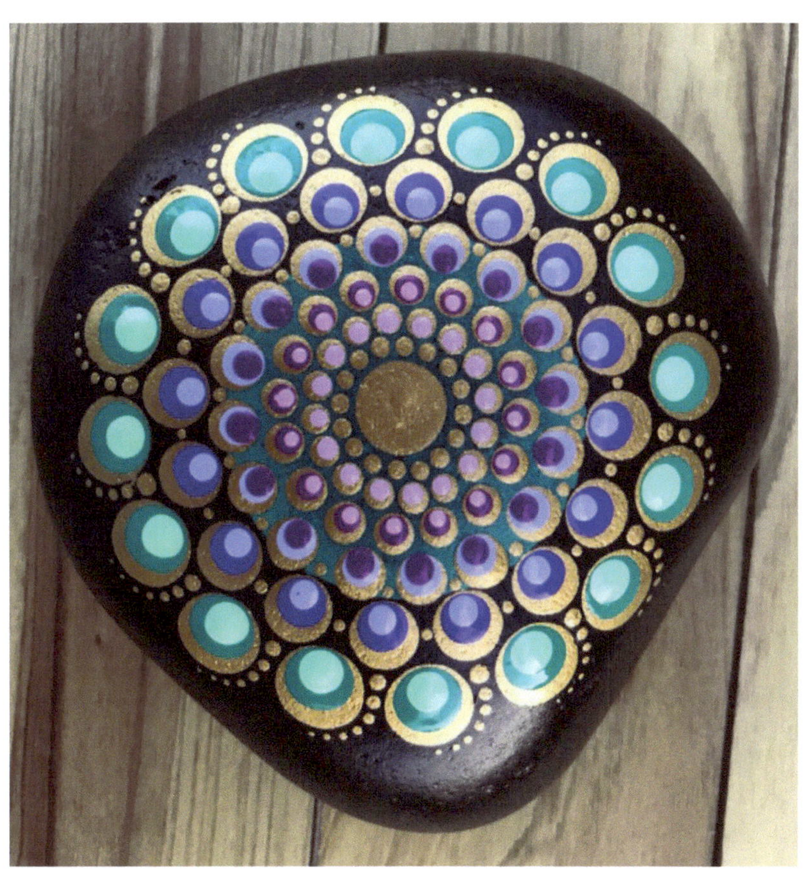

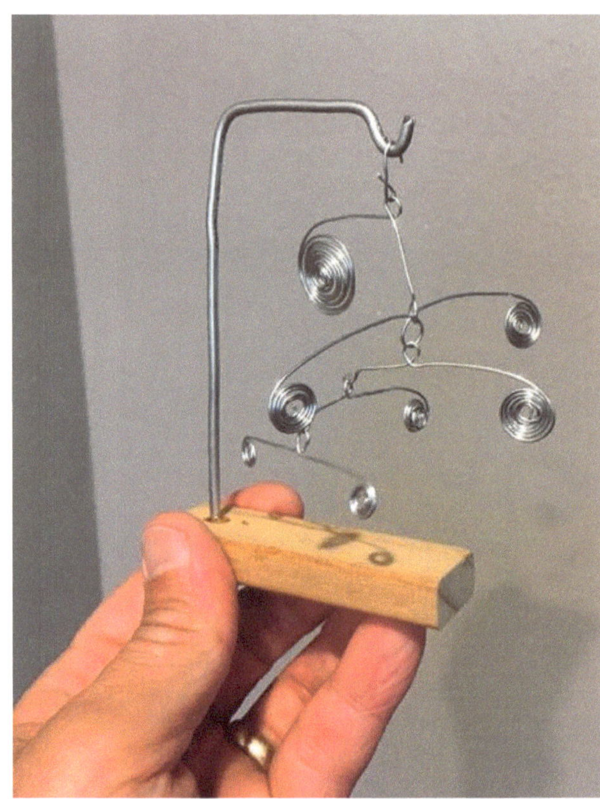

Also, a surprise piece from Allan, a friend from Portland, OR — a wonderful tiny mobile reminiscent of Calder. It will be borrowed often. *A note from early Fall: I Haven't seen it for quite a while, it is obviously being appreciated, and I hope to get pictures from its travels.*

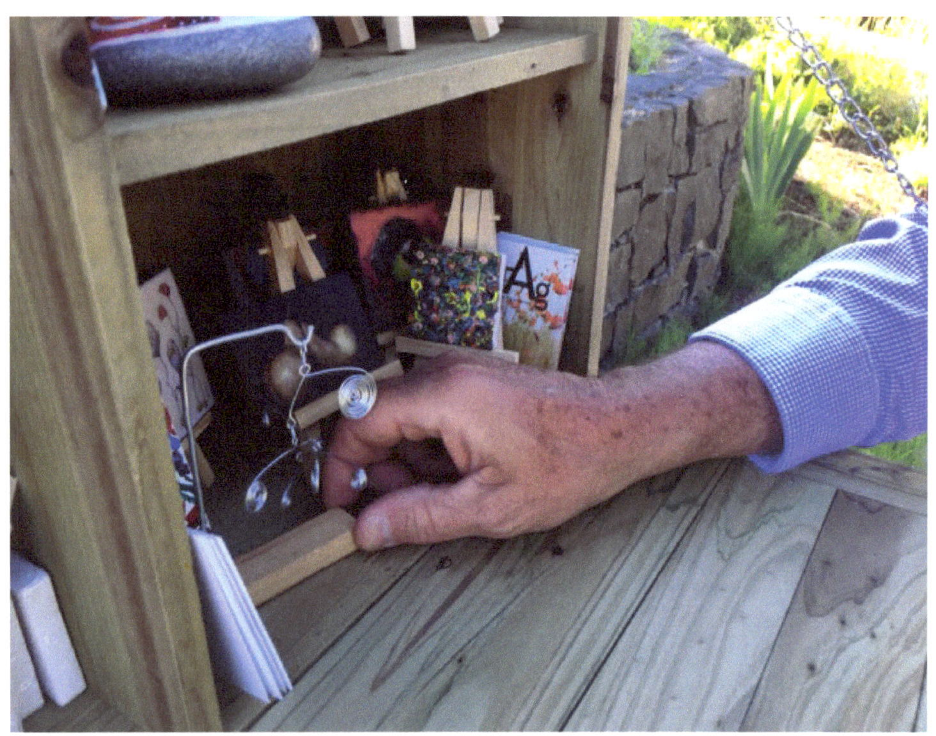

Allan placing his mobile

And then there was, "Snuggling Pears"

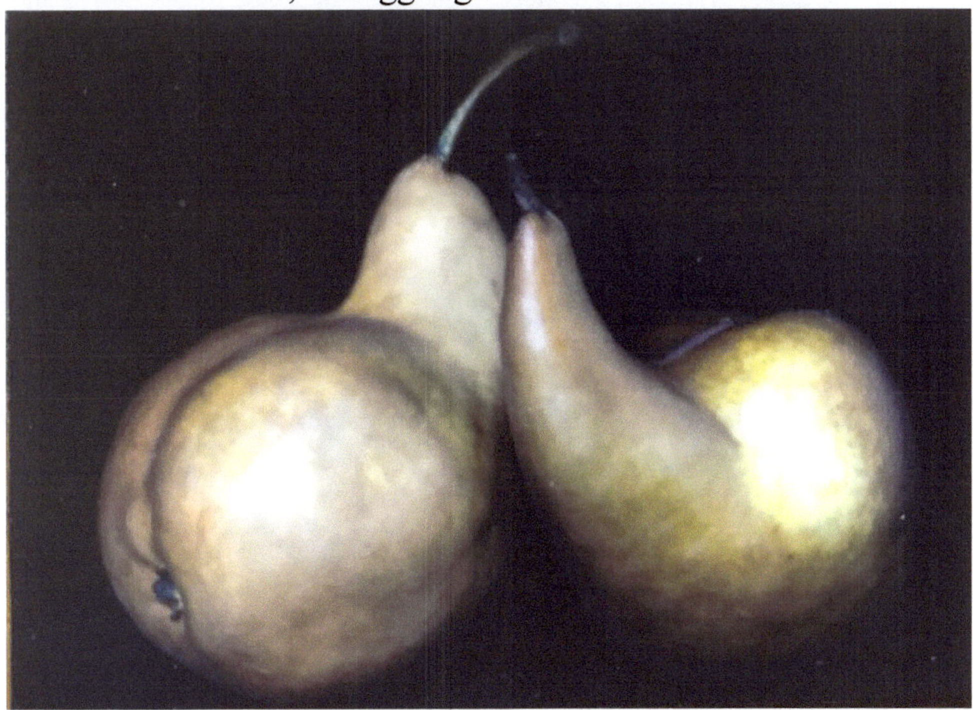

And "Apocalyptic Circus"

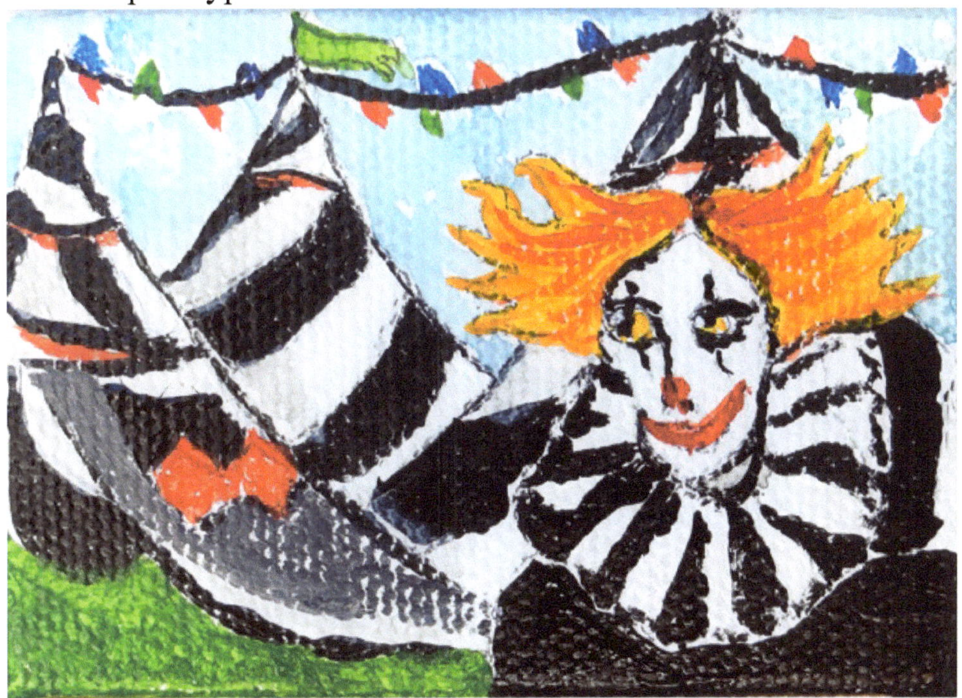

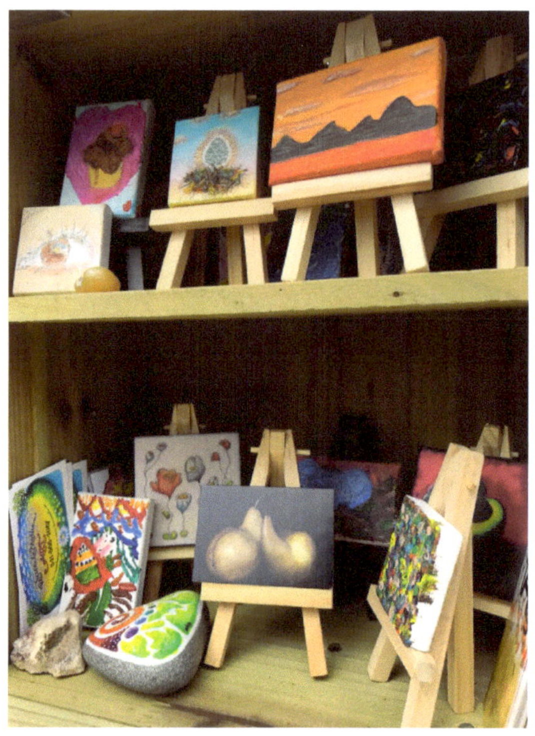

A view of the inside of the TAG = lots of nice pieces.

An eye!

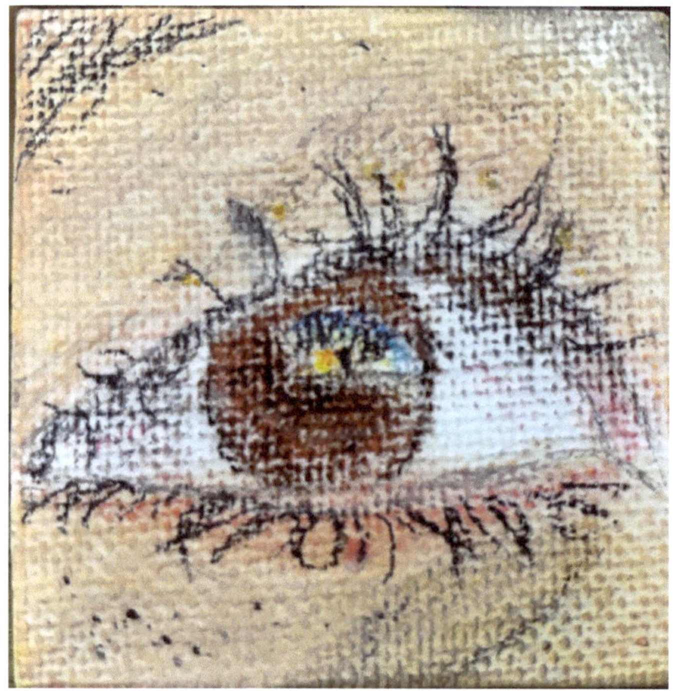

Summer

The 'dog days' of summer are here and it hasn't rained at all for weeks and weeks. The arrival of art has dried up a bit too. However, the flowers are enjoying the sun and growing exuberantly.

Website changes were necessary due to the web service I relied on for photo galleries no longer being available. Cobbling together PHP code resulted in a somewhat dissatisfying gallery page. It also disrupted the saving of images as previously done, necessitating the re-organizing of images into folders on the EJP site. Fortunately, a new FTP software purchase for iPhone has at least restored the ability to take a photo of artwork and upload it to the website fairly easily, hooray!

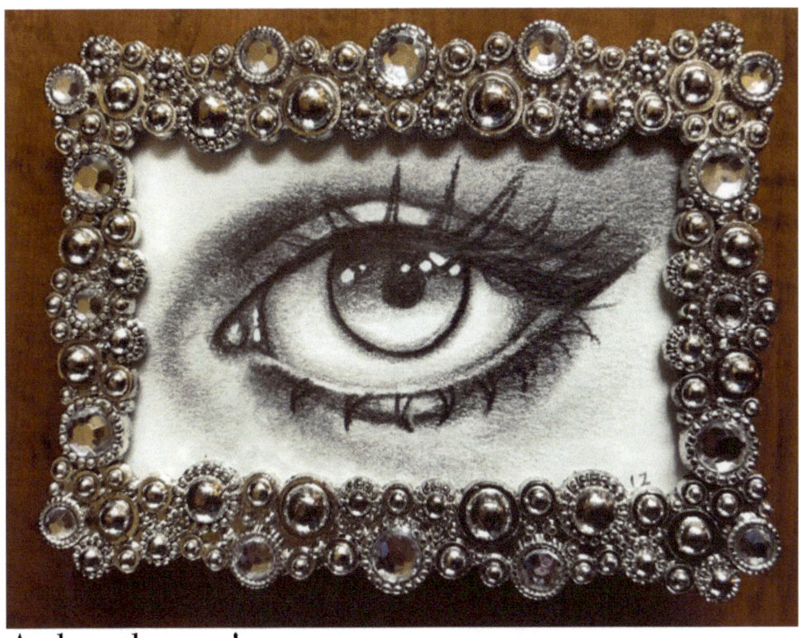

And another eye!

Almost all black.

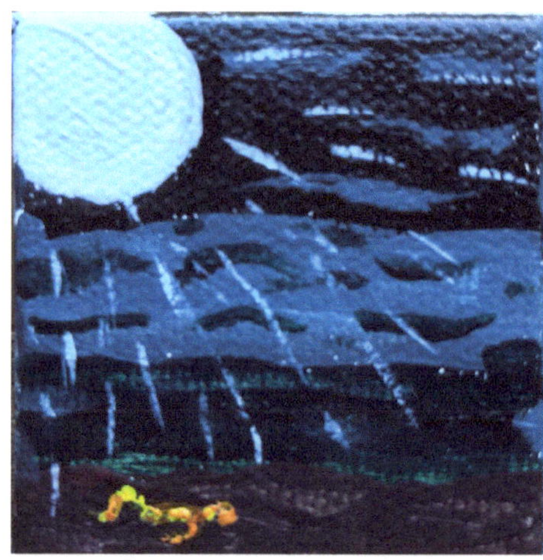

Reaction to the high temperatures?

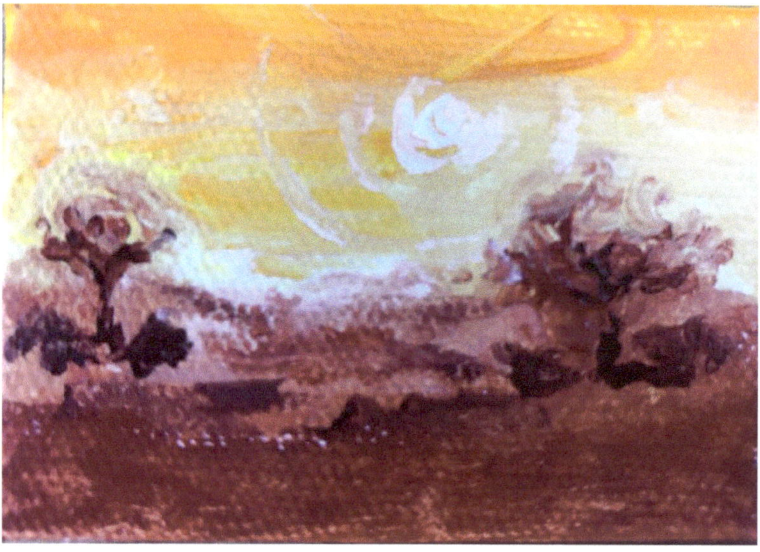

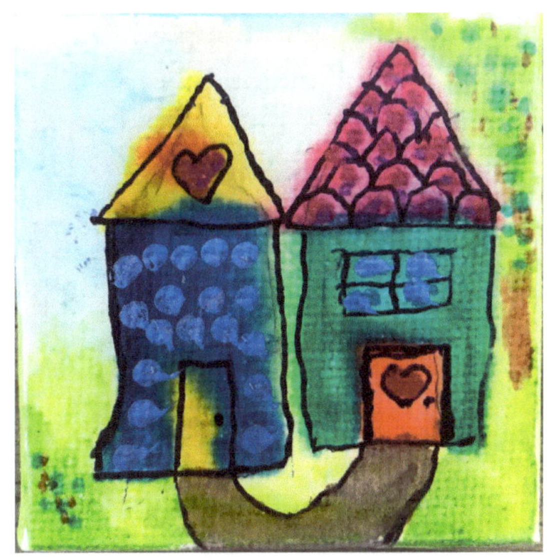

By Sharon
Thank you for supporting the
Tiny Art Gallery!

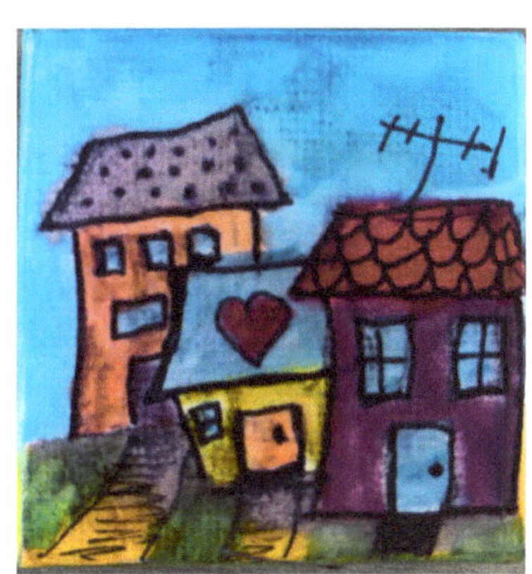

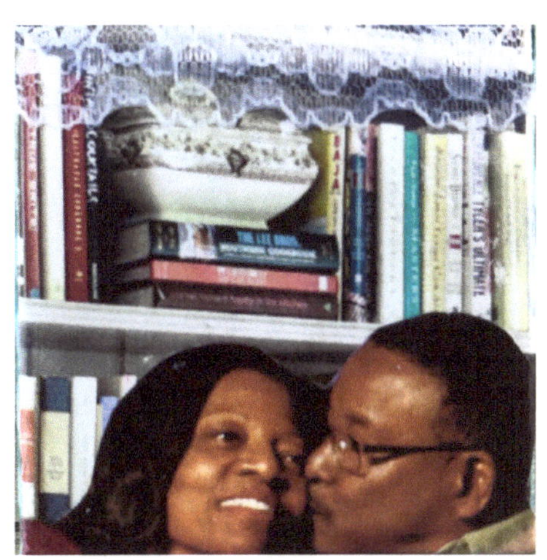

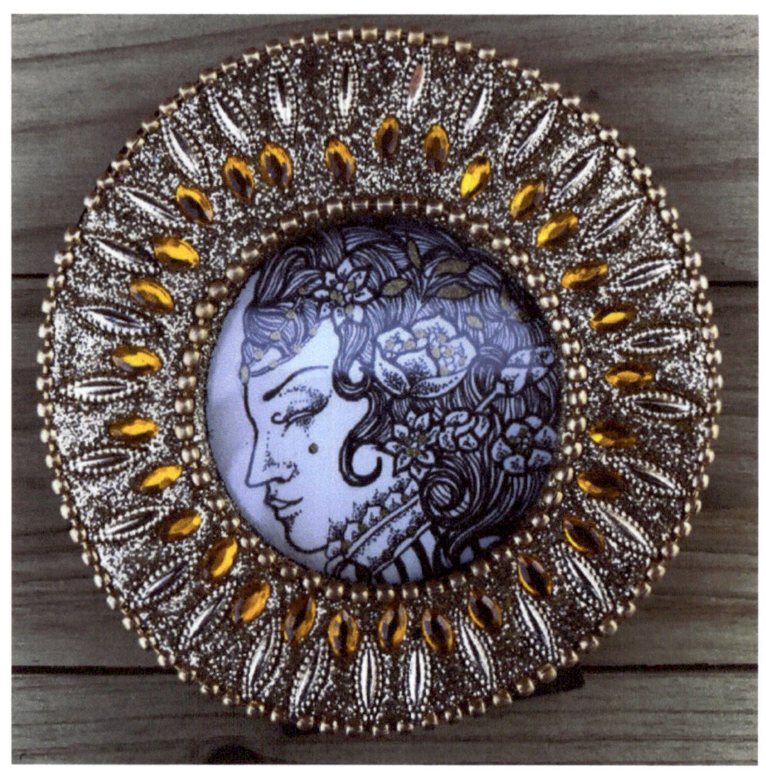

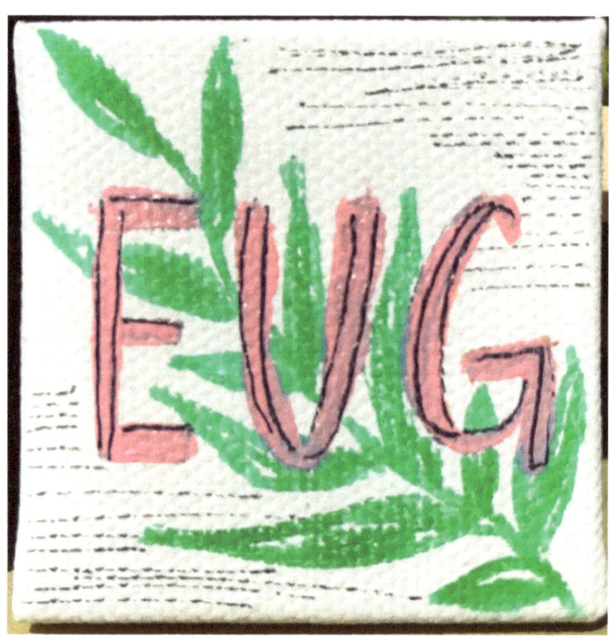

Celebrating Eugene.

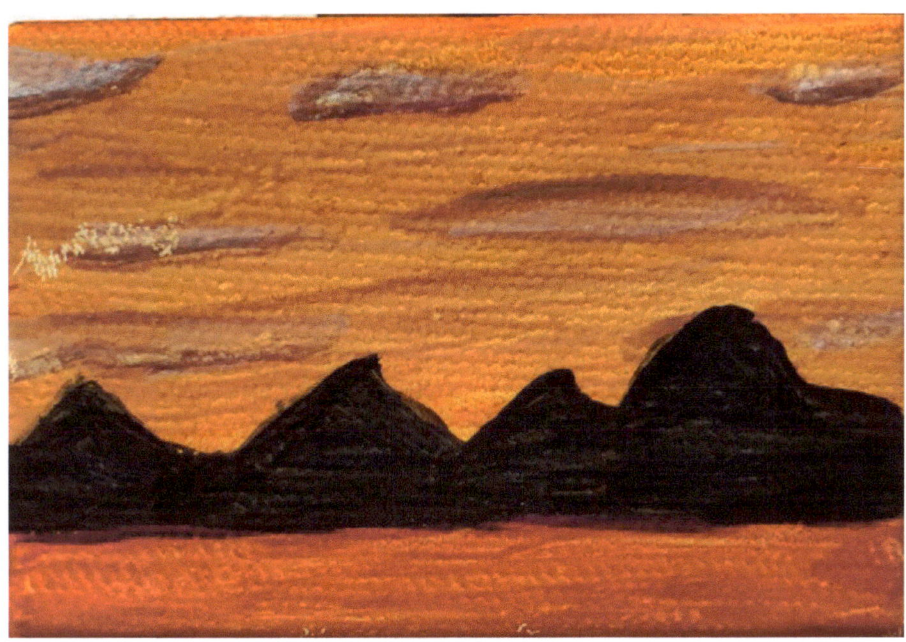

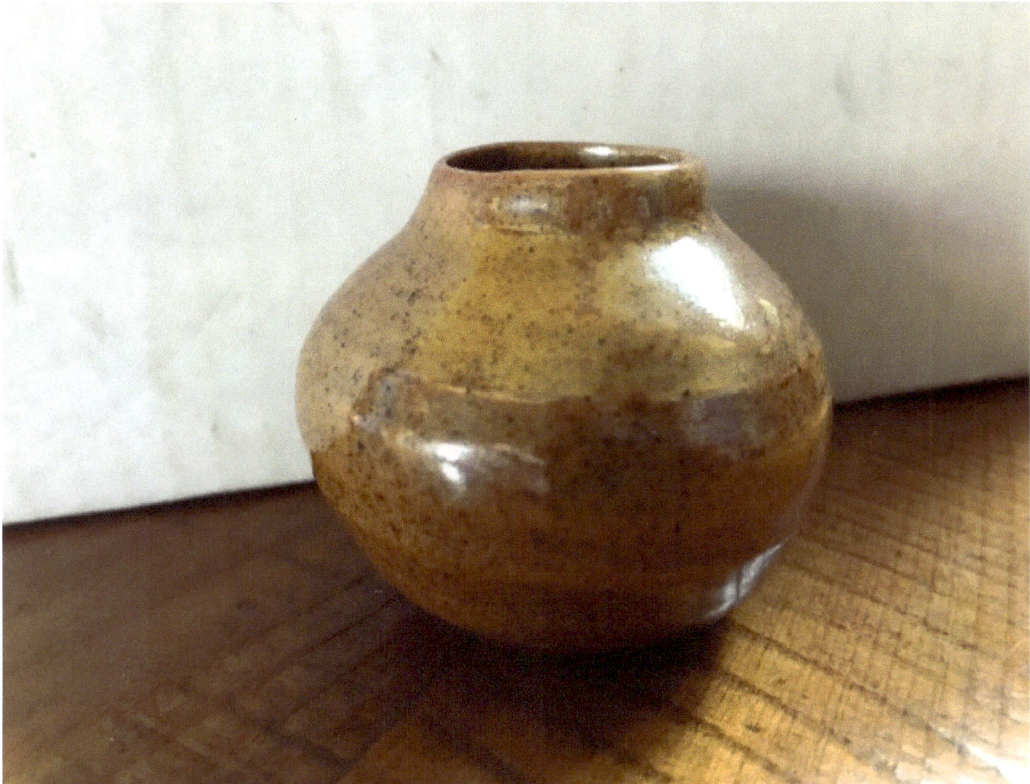

An elegant tiny pot made by John from Portland, OR.

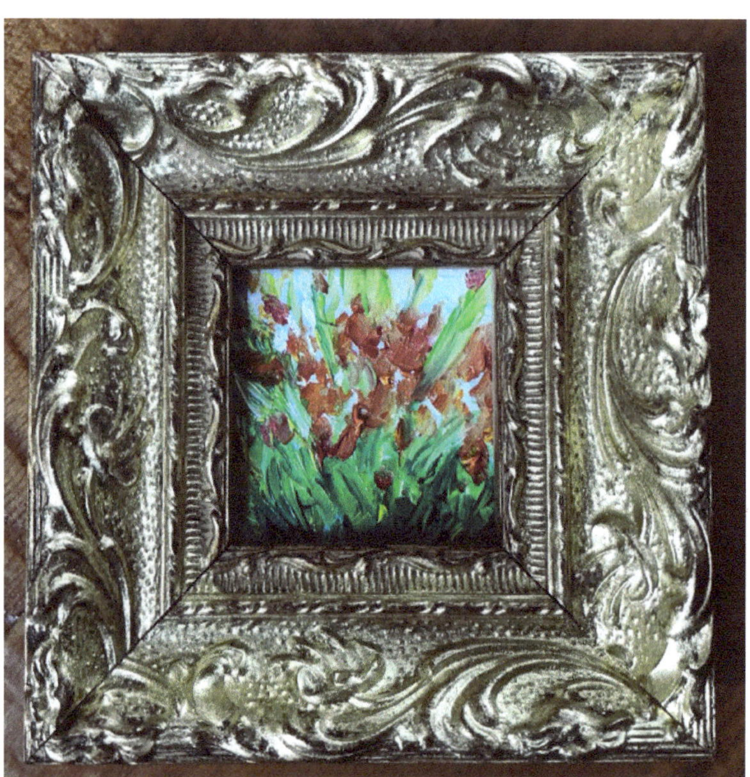

Frame found in a garage sale and donated to the TAG
by Carlos. Shiny new coat of paint added by me.

Earwigs and Artwork

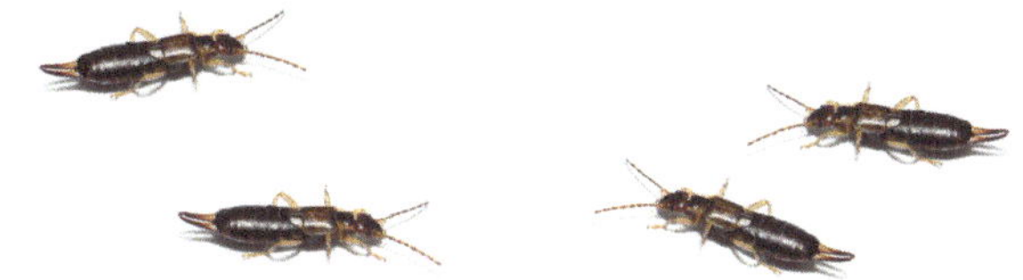

The early morning check of the Tiny Art Gallery sometimes produces a nice surprise of new art. Occasionally, there are little guests taking a morning tour of the art, or just waking up from staying overnight. Earwigs are the most common visitor to the TAG. They tend to scatter when the door is opened, but sometimes will group together and 'hide'.

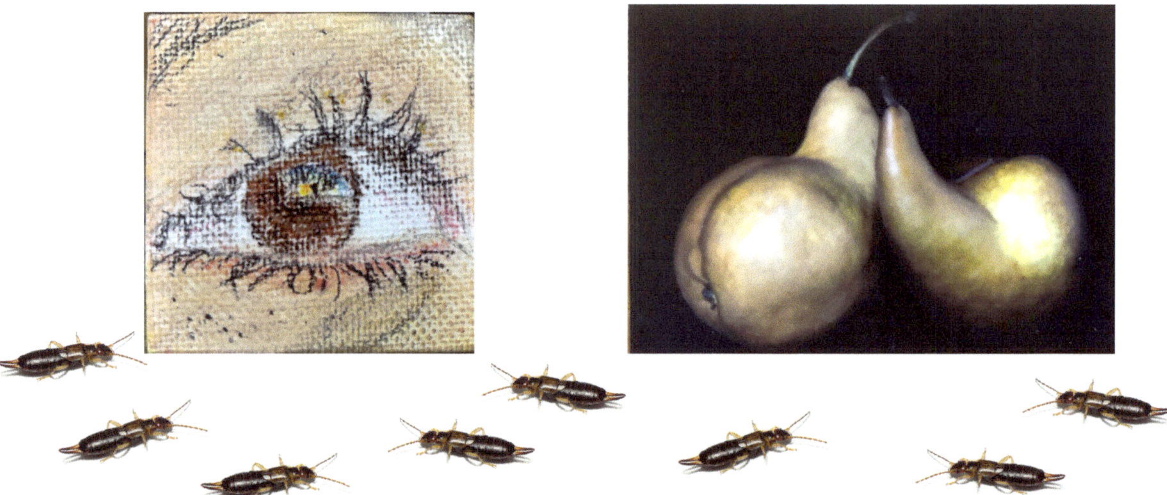

Nearing the End
of Summer

    Squirrels eat the sunflowers like Sumo preparing for a winter match. They don't seem interested in art, but neighbors have been mentioning and showing the Gallery to others and word is spreading.

    I met the youngest (known) artist with art in the Gallery - Nate, age 2. His work, a wonderful abstract red smear that any practiced artist would be proud of.

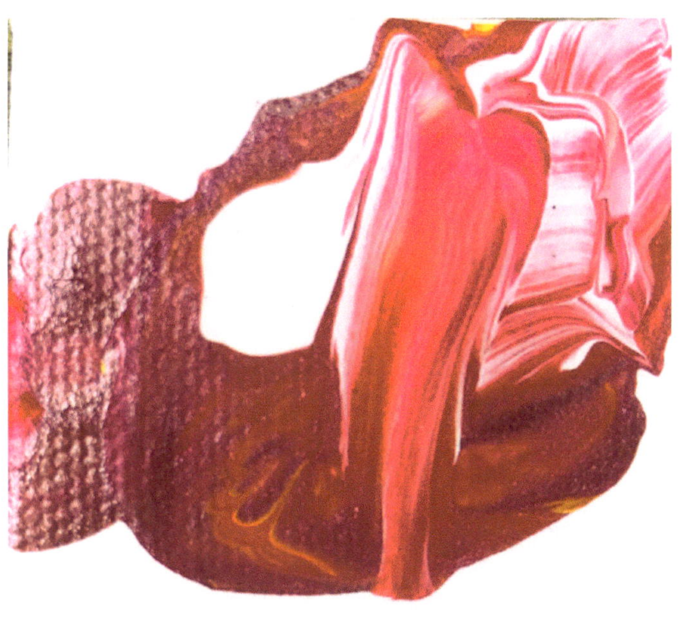

The rains are back and so are the cooler evenings. Fall is in the air. And then it is 90°F, that's Summer in Oregon.

I've started working on a piece of art for the front of the TAG. It's going to be pastel on paper encased in resin. I decided it was time, after talking with a few people who were reluctant to investigate the unknown box. The art should clarify and hopefully invite more investigation. The local newspaper got back in touch and is interested in running a piece on the TAG. Interview set up. Front artwork should be ready — just in time.

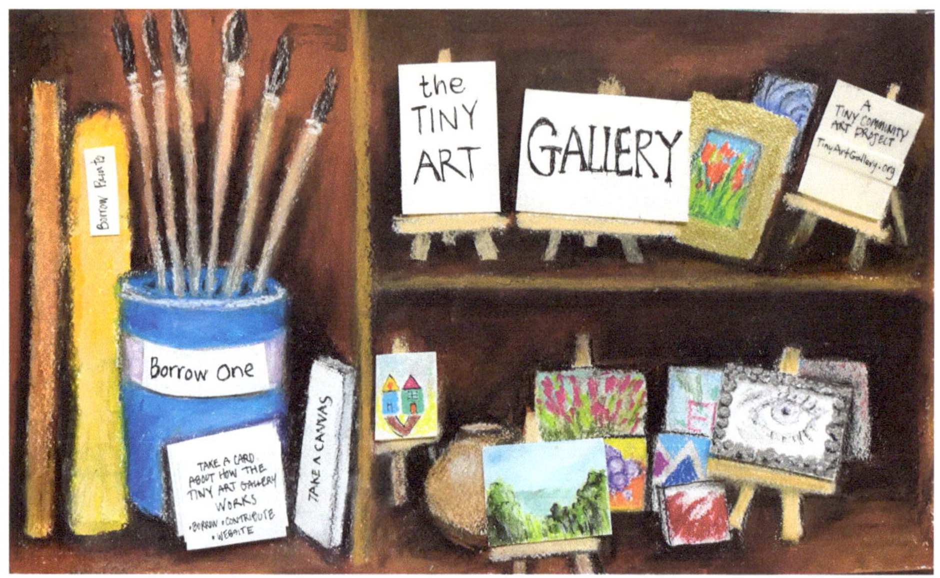

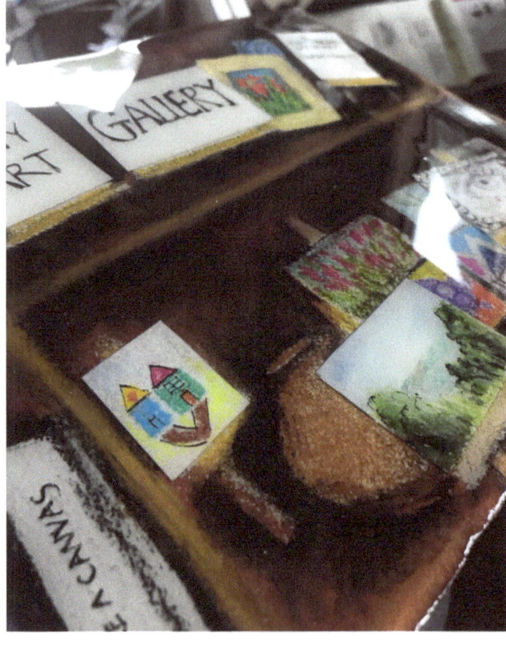

Resin coated.

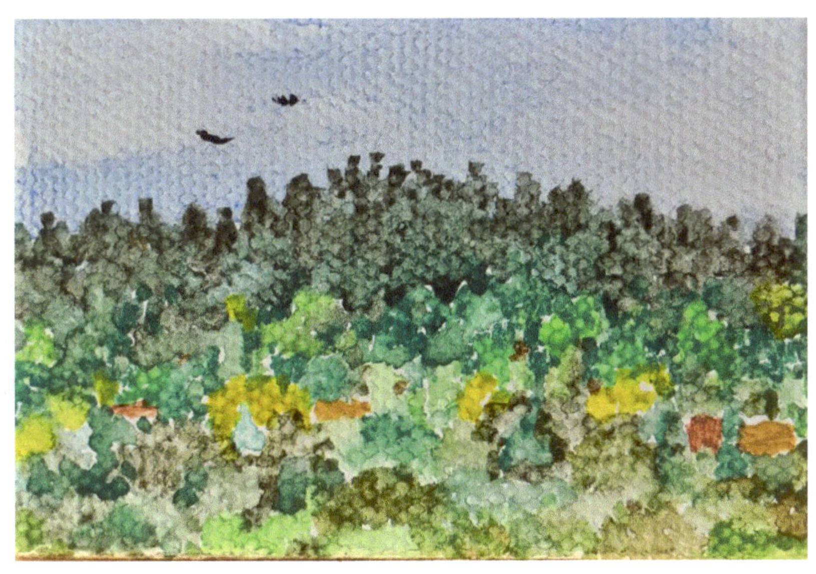

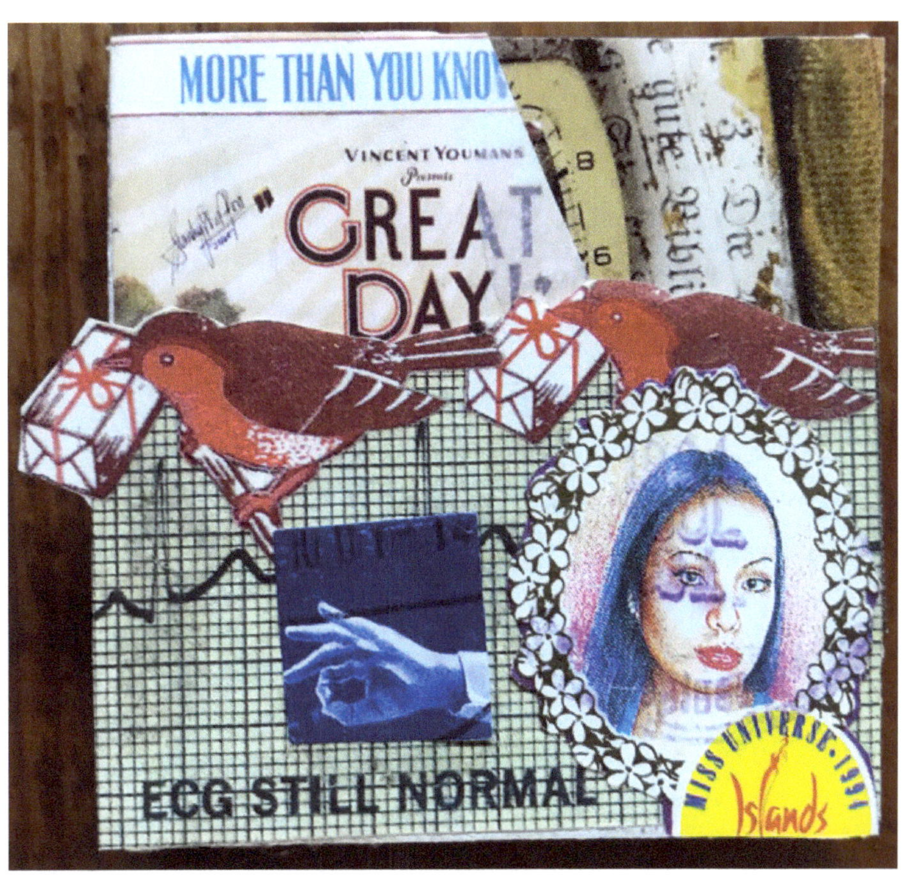
MORE THAN YOU KNOW
VINCENT YOUMANS
Presents
"GREAT DAY!"
Die Bibli
8
6
ECG STILL NORMAL
MISS UNIVERSE · 1999
Islands

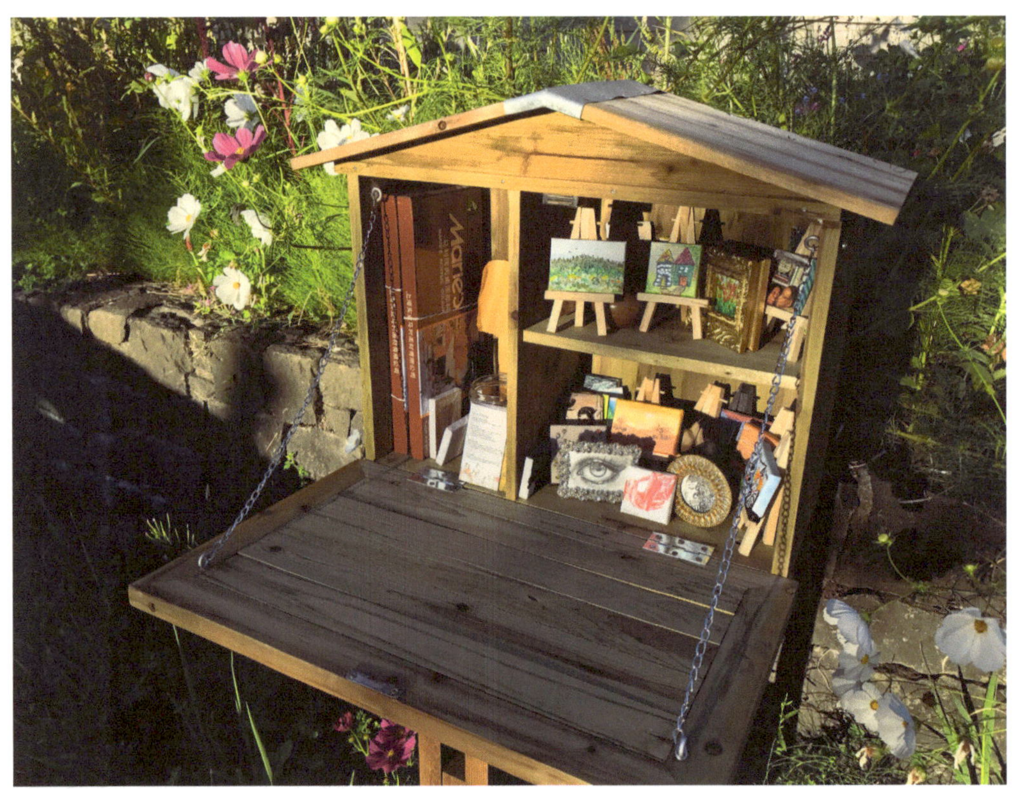

October to the Publication of the Book

The rain subsided for a few days, and I was finally able to meet with Kelly the photographer from the local paper - The Register Guard. We had a nice photo shoot in the brisk sunny morning. About a week later I was interviewed by Kirsten Williams of the Register Guard for the piece. She later informed me that, after researching, the Tiny Art Gallery is likely the smallest art gallery in the Oregon, and possibly the United States. That's pretty interesting! The story about the Tiny Art Gallery was on Sunday, October 22nd. Here is the link: goo.gl/bE8ZF6

More canvases and paints were borrowed the morning of the photo shoot, and I'm looking forward to seeing what is made. New pieces haven't been put in the Gallery for at least a week. I imagine it has to do with the start of school.

A side note, the use of resin to seal the image for the front of the TAG has me thinking of using resin more in my personal artwork. I will use the small size of the TAG pieces for experiments, and they will probably end up in the Gallery. An interesting dynamic - showing small experiments that may lead to larger works.

I put out the word that the book will be finishing up and people should make art in the next week or two if they wanted it in the book. All the art supplies were borrowed, so we'll see what fun things return, unfortunately they'll have to be in the next book because this one needs to go to press. I hope you've found the process of starting the Tiny Art Gallery interesting, and enjoyed the artwork.

Artwork Borrowed From the TAG and Shown at Home

The following images represent a piece of art borrowed from the Tiny Art Gallery and displayed, usually in an interesting context. It has been fun to see what people pair with the art. I have done a few of these, too. **Enjoy.**

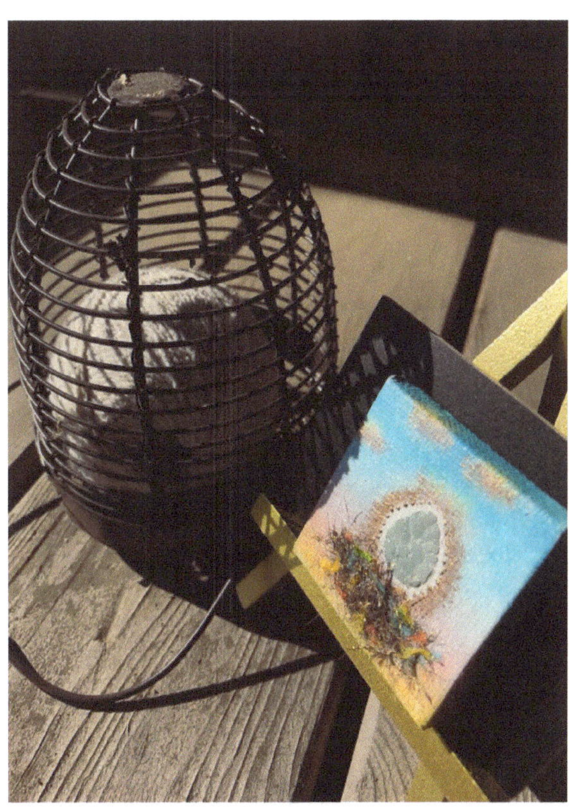

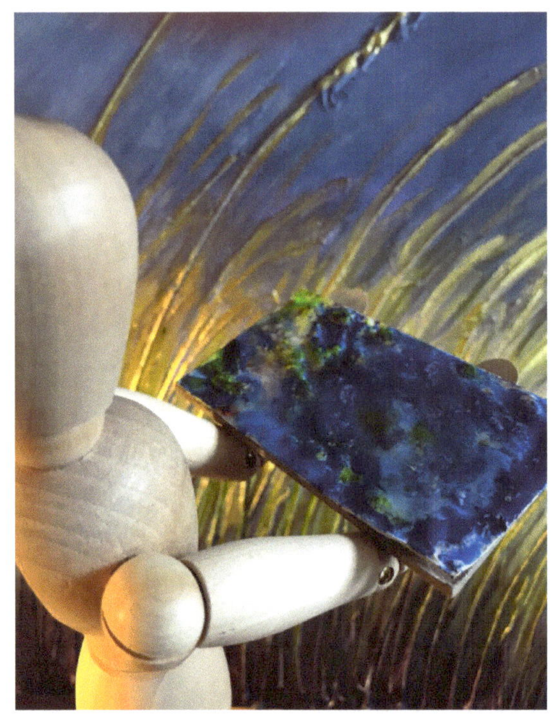

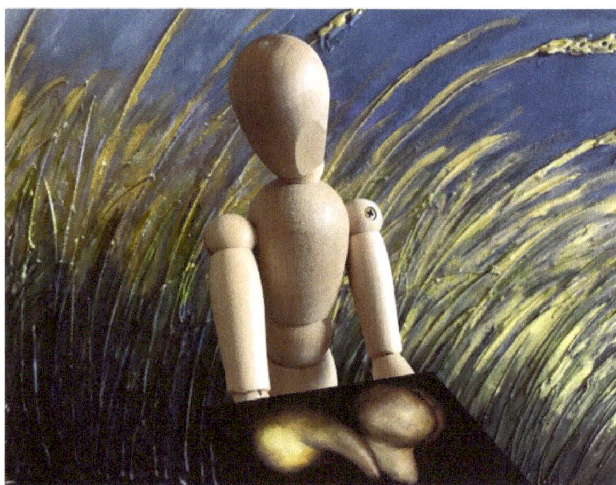

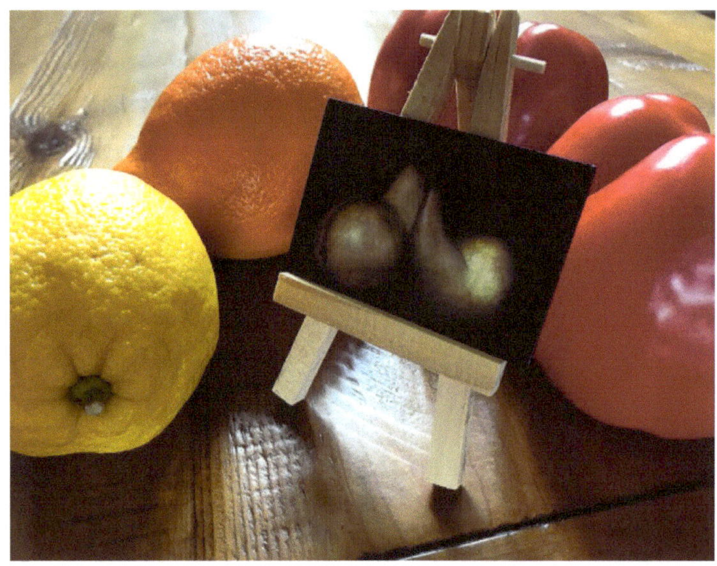

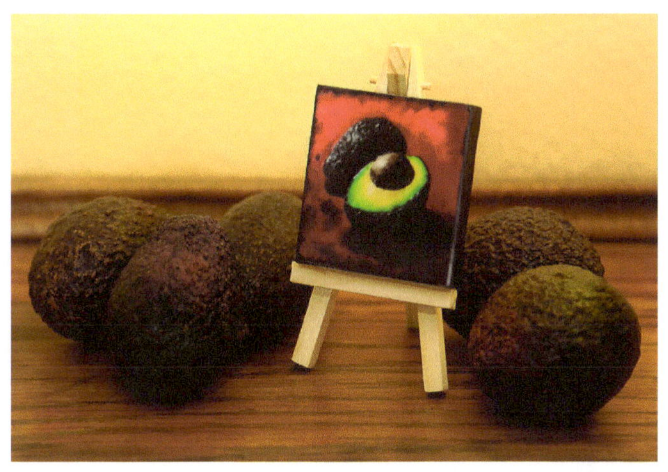

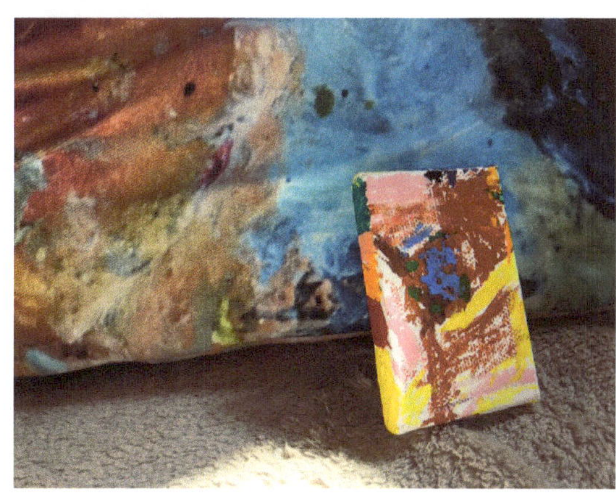

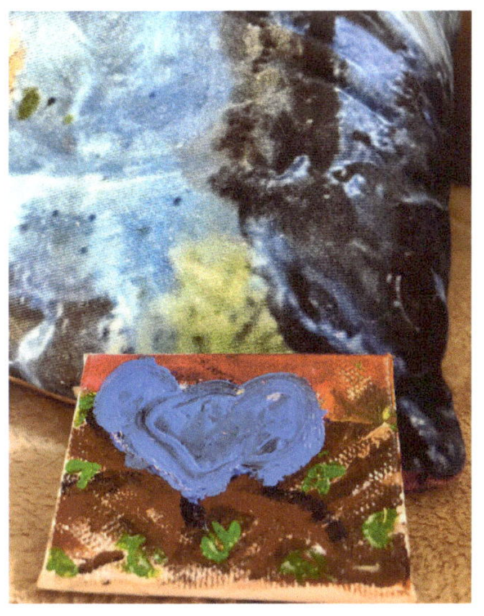

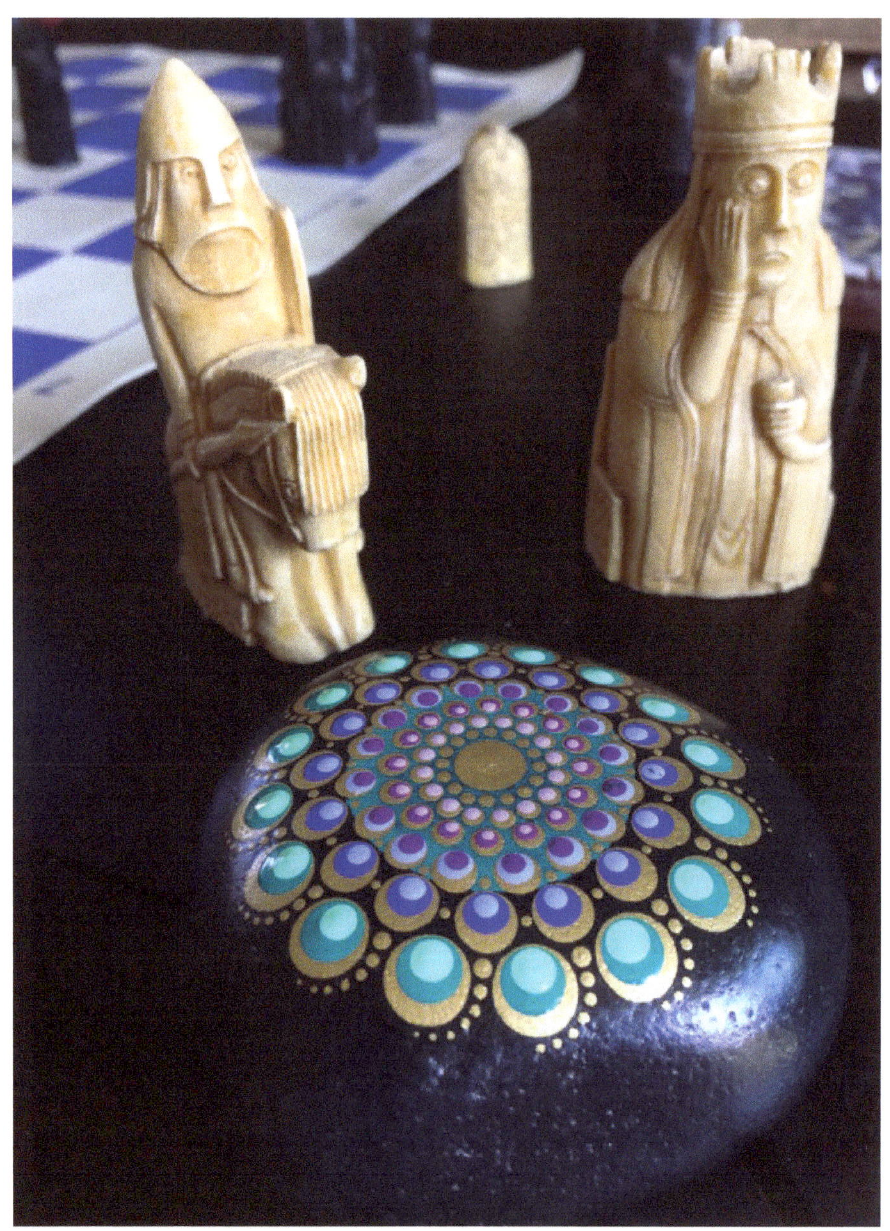

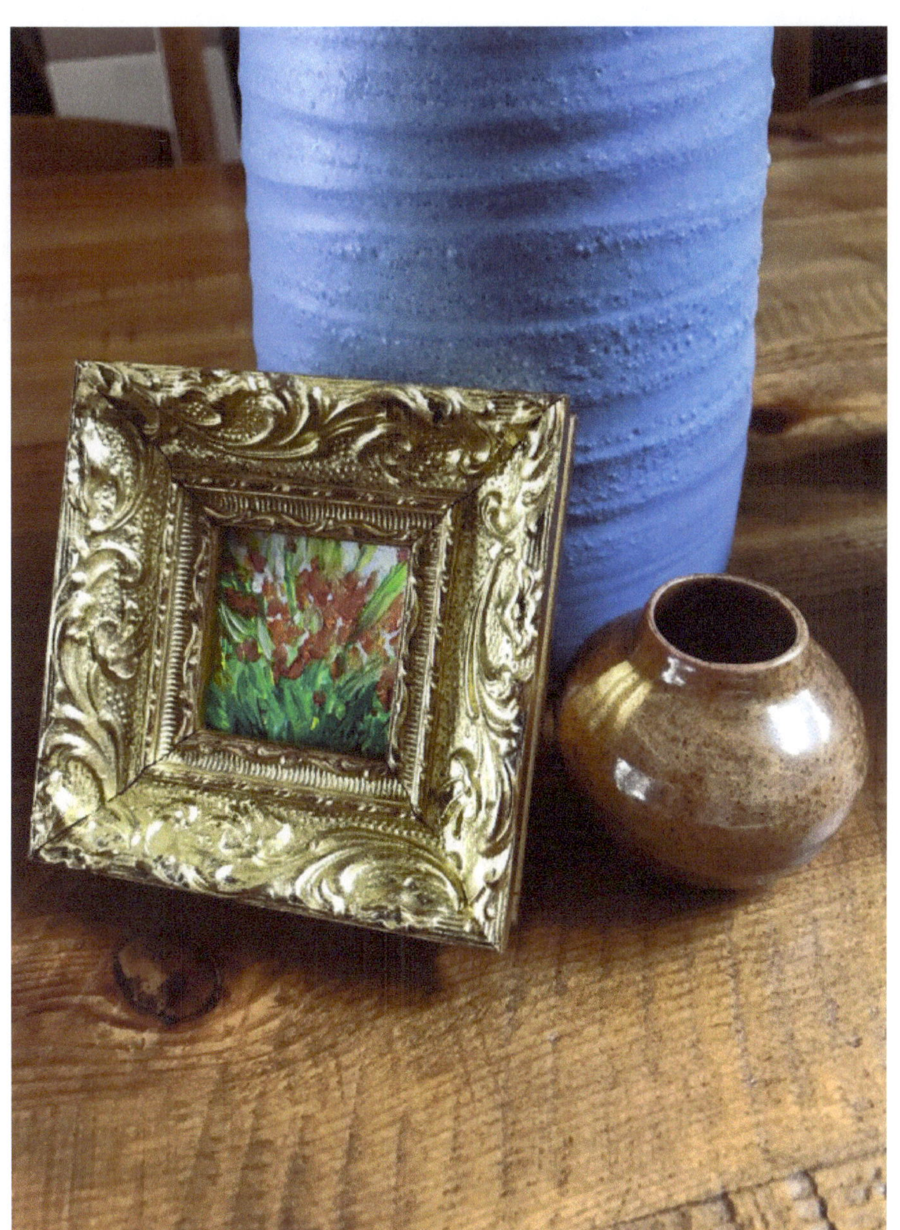

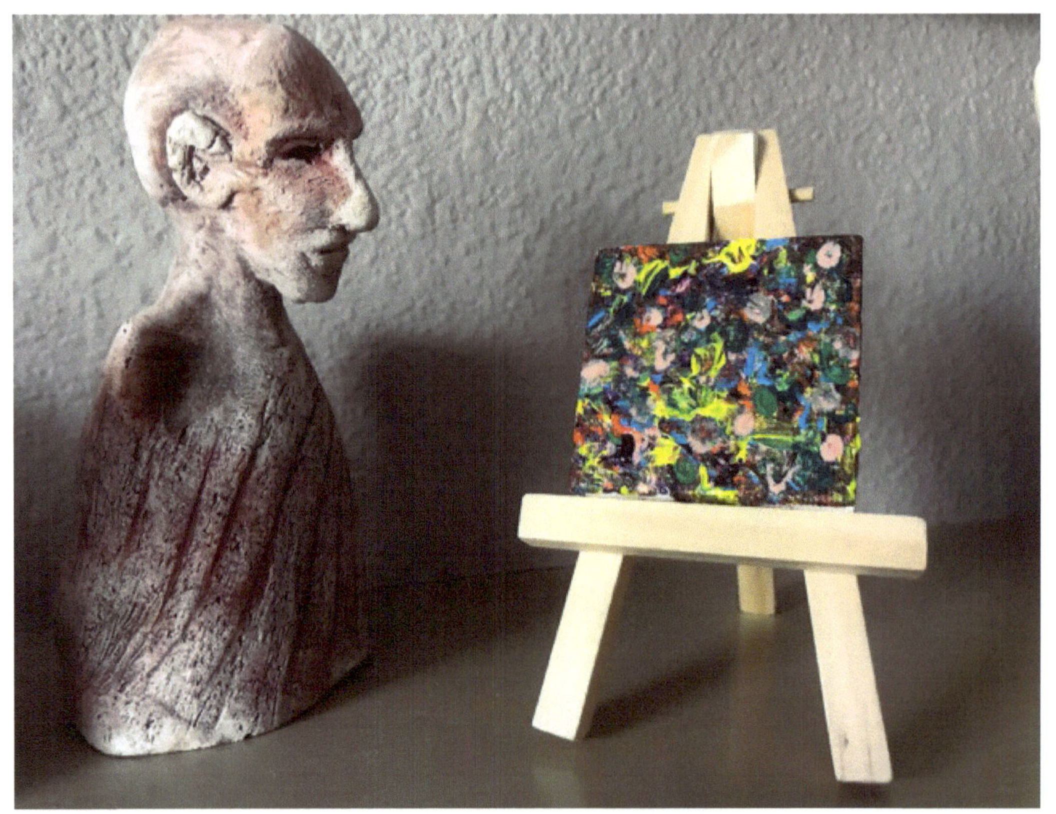

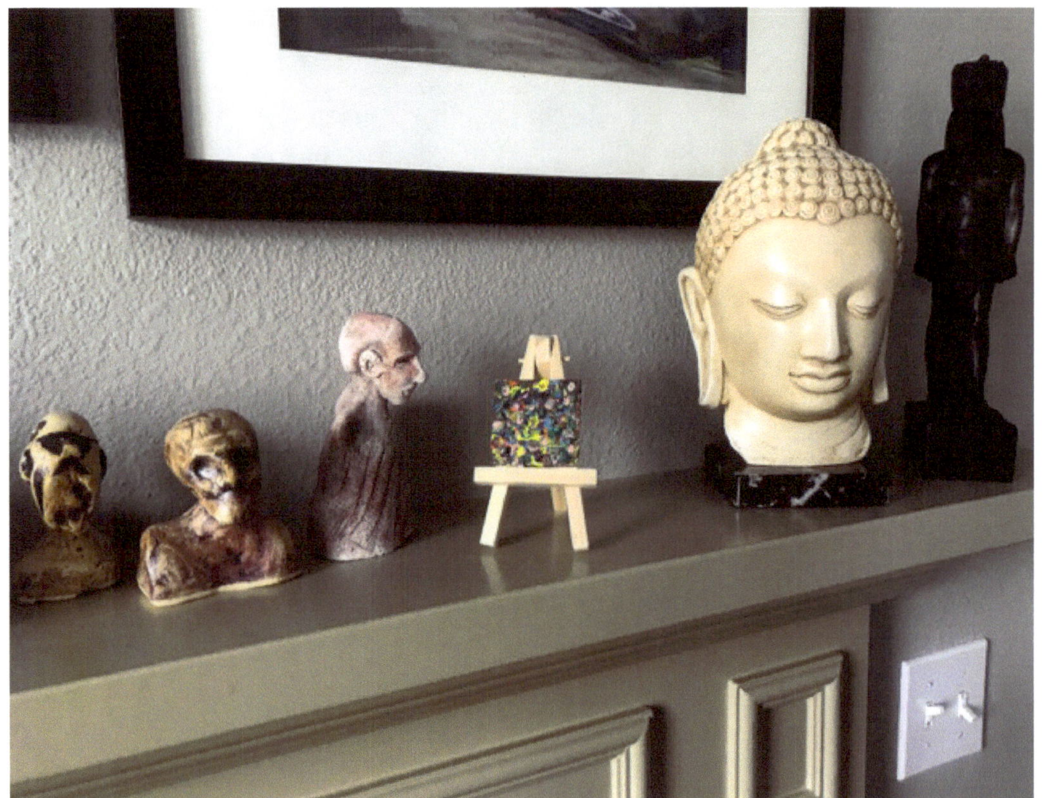

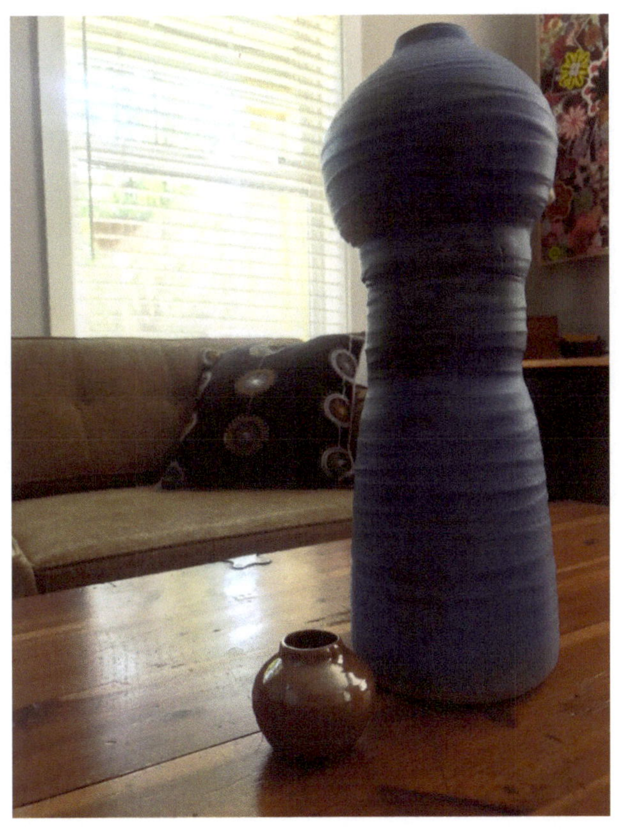

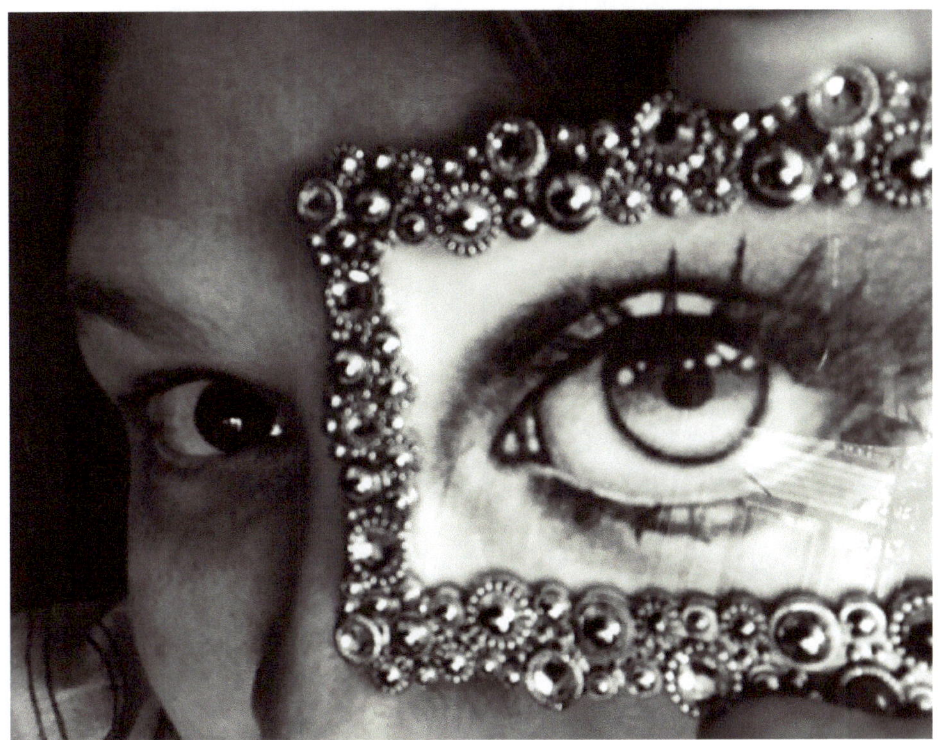

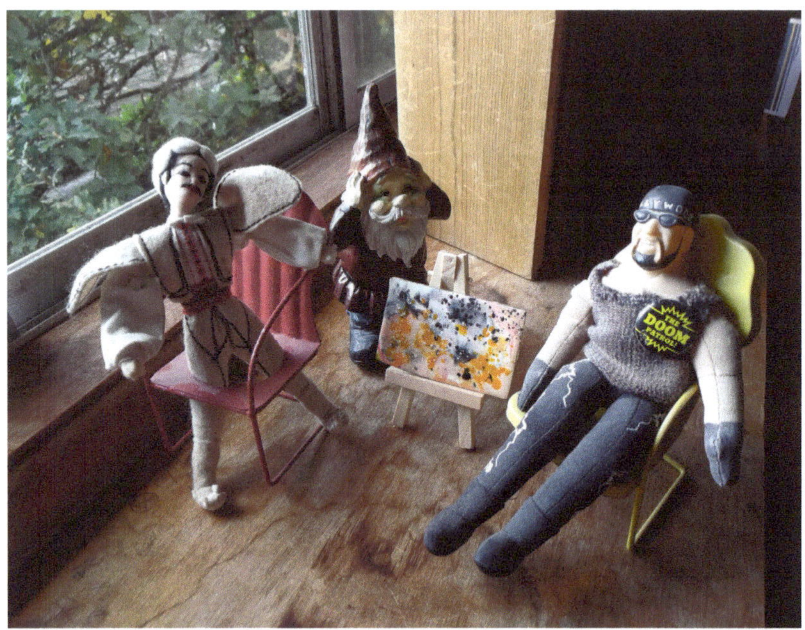

Enjoying 'Abstract Koi' at home.

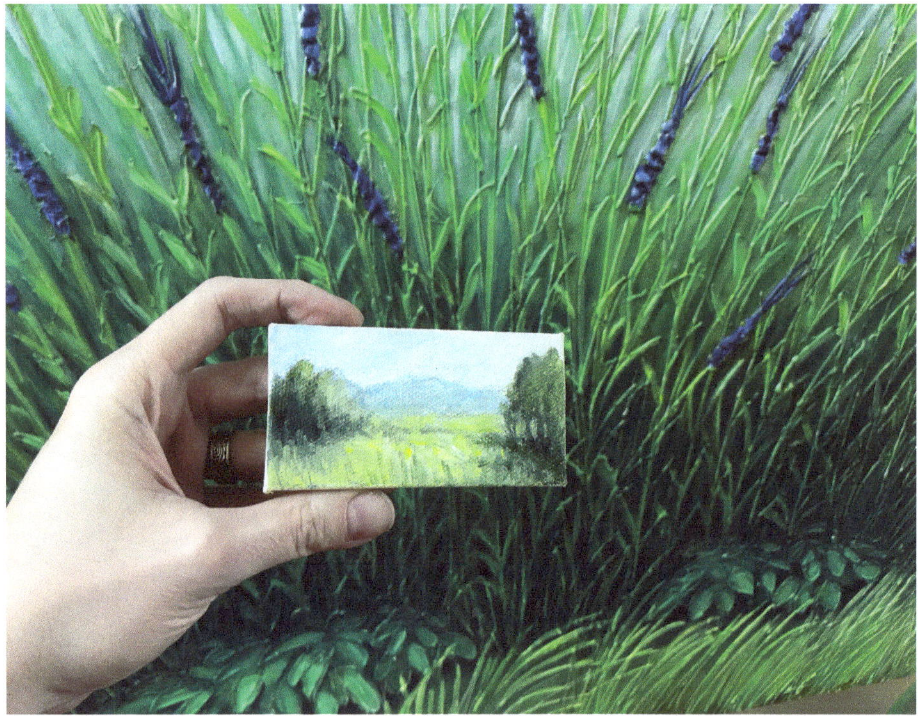

Big and tiny.

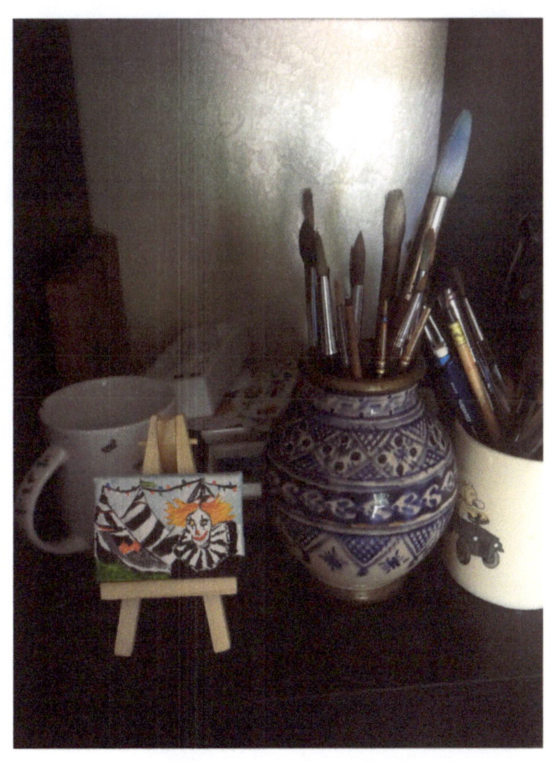

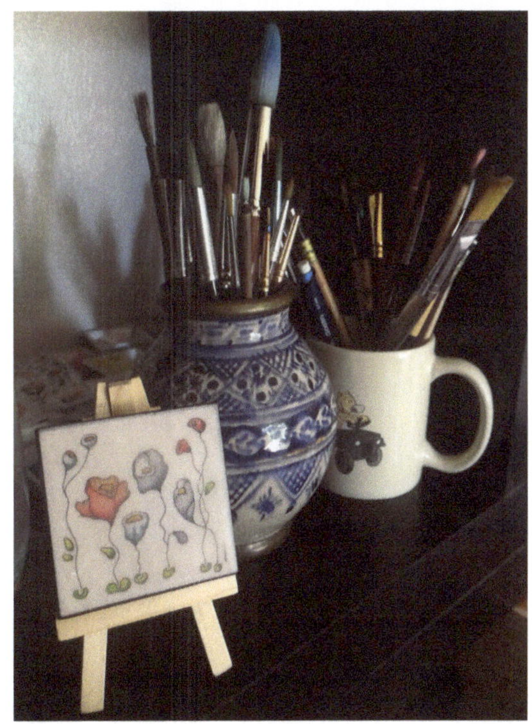

After-word

This project has been a rewarding experience. From the initial idea, to the positive feedback from neighbors, all the interesting artwork that people have made, to the article in the newspaper and then the completion of this book. The TAG has been a way to meet neighbors that I wouldn't normally meet – it's a great conversation starter. And watching people discover the Tiny Art Gallery for the first time, or show a friend or family member is wonderful.

I enjoy looking at what people have been doing in the TAG – leaving art, borrowing art, and organizing! This is something I had not anticipated, people seem to be looking after the new tiny addition to their neighborhood. Hopefully the next year will be as interesting and creative as the last. The piece in the newspaper may increase the visibility of the Gallery, hopefully only in good ways.

The Tiny Art Gallery idea has become a functioning gallery. I'm going to continue improving and refining the space, surroundings, and the website. There will also be a book next year with the latest art and commentary about what is going on with the TAG. Maybe the next book will include works from people beyond the state of Oregon (hint). If you want to arrange something like that, send an email.

What will the Gallery look like with snow on it? What about battery powered string lights? Will the transplanted sage proliferate and make a nice backdrop for the Gallery? Will the squirrels be able to eat all the sunflowers I plant next spring?

Stay tuned for the next year of The Tiny Art Gallery.

TinyArtGallery.org
tag@ecojusticepress.com